MATHS PRACTICE PAPERS
FOR SENIOR SCHOOL ENTRY

PETER ROBSON

INTRODUCTION

The ten papers in this book are for practice in the kinds of questions you could be asked in Year 7 (11+) senior school entrance exams.

There is no time limit for each paper. The idea is to try to arrive at the correct answers.

Entrance exams vary greatly from school to school. Some will ask easier questions than the ones in this book; some will ask harder ones. If your chosen school issues past papers, make sure you try them. Many of them are available online.

If you want to estimate your percentage marks for each paper, award yourself 3 marks for each correctly answered complete question from questions 1 to 20, and 4 marks for each question from 21 to 30.

The topics covered in the book are listed inside the back cover.

EQUIPMENT NEEDED

Pencil and eraser.
Ruler, for drawing straight lines.

As no measuring is required, geometrical instruments are not needed and are not likely to help you to answer the questions.

Calculators should NOT be used.

SOME MATHEMATICAL WORDS USED IN THE BOOK

It is useful to know the meanings of these words before you attempt the papers:-

area	even	radius
circumference	hexagon	rectangle
column	increase	reflection
consecutive	intersection	regular
cube	kite	rhombus
cube root	odd	rotation
cuboid	parallel	row
decrease	parallelogram	square
diagonal	pentagon	square root
diameter	percentage	sum
difference	perimeter	symmetry
digit	prime	trapezium
divisible	product	triangle

CONTENTS

ANSWER BOOK

There is a separate answer book
'Maths Practice Papers. Answers and Explanations'
published by Newby Books (ISBN 1-978-872686-40-0).

(BLANK PAGE)

1.
```
    3 8 4
+   7 2 7
―――――――――
```

2.
```
  1 1 9 4
−   6 3 9
―――――――――
```

3.
```
    1 9 2
×     4 4
―――――――――
```

4. Find 74% of 900.

5. Write in figures: three hundred and five thousand and thirty five.

6. A prize of £3 760 is shared equally among 20 people. How much does each person receive?

7. Work out the sum of 16·17, 6·096 and 4

8. A family travelled to Melbury Bay for their holidays. They set off at 9.40 a.m. and their journey took $3\frac{3}{4}$ hours. At what time did they arrive at Melbury Bay?

____

9. There are 75 sweets on the left side of the balance, and 23 on the right. How many sweets must be moved from left to right to make both sides equal?

____

10. Put these in order of size, starting with the largest.

$$\frac{1}{5} \quad , \quad 0{\cdot}23 \quad , \quad 28\% \quad , \quad 0{\cdot}027 \quad , \quad 2{\cdot}2$$

____

11.

Three cards are numbered 6 , 3 and 9. In what order must they be placed to give

    (a) the highest possible number ?

____

    (b) the lowest possible even number ?

____

    (c) a number divisible by 7 ?

____

12. Write the next two numbers in each of these sequences.

    (a) 54 , 42 , 30 , 18 , _________ , _________

    (b) 3 , 9 , 27 , _________ , _________

13. Ahmed buys   2 small pizzas at 92p each
                      2 bags of chips at £2.25 a bag
                      1 bottle of fruit juice at 99p

    (a) How much does he spend altogether?

                                   ____

    (b) He pays with a £10 note. How much change should he receive?

                                   ____

14. The longer side of a rectangle is 9 cm and its area is 63 cm^2. What is its perimeter?

                                   ____

15.

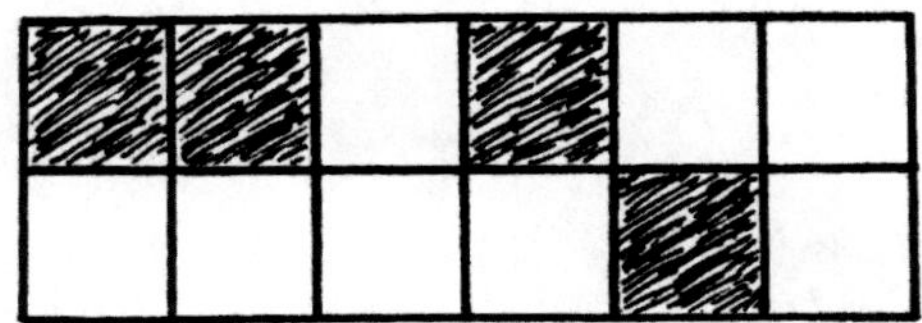

(a) What fraction of this figure is shaded? Give your answer in its simplest form.

                                   ____

(b) How many more squares need to be shaded so that only $\frac{1}{4}$ of the figure remains unshaded?

                                   ____

16. Bromine melts at -7° C.   Mercury melts at -39° C.   Potassium melts at $+64^\circ$ C.

    (a) Which of these elements has the lowest melting point?

    ____

    (b) What is the difference in temperature between the highest and lowest melting points of the three elements?

    ____

17. If $f = 4$, $g = 3$ and $h = 6$, calculate the value of

    (i) $4f + \dfrac{h}{g}$

    ____

    (ii) $5 (h + f - g)$

    ____

    (iii) $h^2 - f^2$

    ____

18.

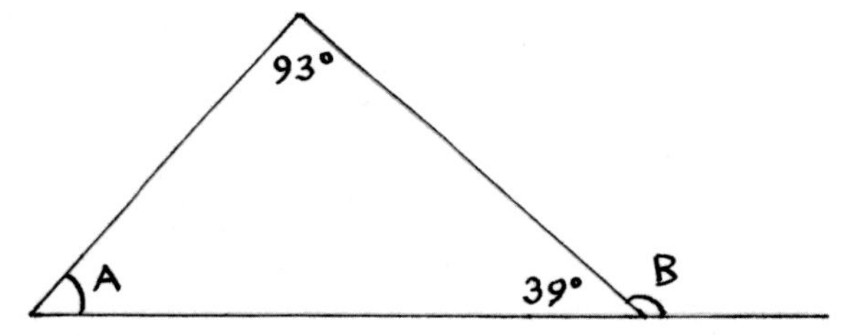

Find the sizes of angles A and B (not drawn to scale).

Angle A

    ____

Angle B

    ____

19. The hours of sunshine (to the nearest hour) recorded in a town during one week were

Sunday 3, Monday 5, Tuesday 9, Wednesday 1, Thursday 0, Friday 3, Saturday 7.

What was the average (mean) daily amount of sunshine?

    ____

20.

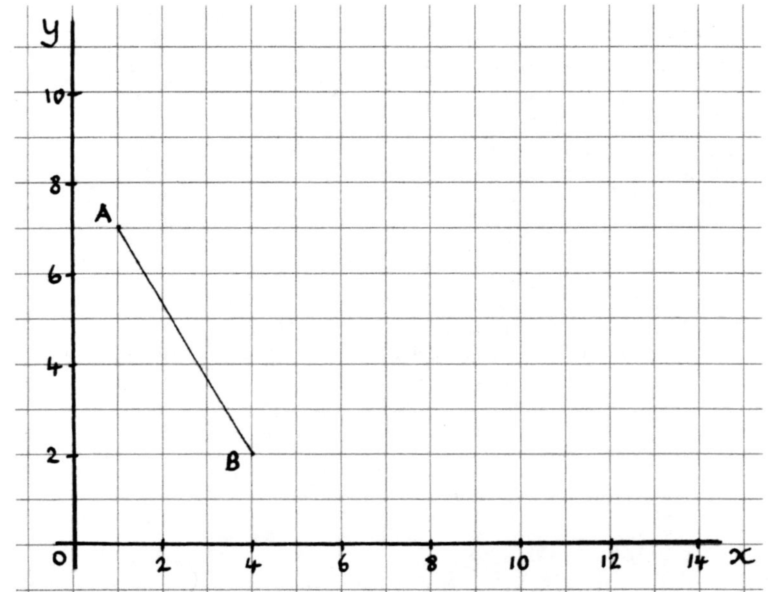

The grid shows point A with coordinates (1 , 7) and point B (4 , 2) and straight line AB.

On the grid, mark points C (13 , 4) and D (6 , 10). Join with straight lines AD, DC and BC.

   (a) What kind of shape is ABCD?

   (b) Inside the shape, what kind of angle is at point A?

   (c) What are the coordinates of the intersection of the diagonals of the shape?

21. The difference between 3^2 and 2^2 is 5
     The difference between 12^2 and 11^2 is 23

Find the difference between

(i) 23^2 and 22^2

(ii) 199^2 and 200^2

(iii) a^2 and $(a - 1)^2$

(iv) $(-78)^2$ and $(-77)^2$

22. There are 37 tourists at a café. They all order either a sandwich or a cake or both.

25 order a sandwich; 30 order a cake

(a) How many order both?

____

(b) How many order a sandwich but not a cake?

____

23. The day of the month when Ben was born is a prime number, has 2 digits, and is 2 more than a square number. On which day of the month was he born?

____

24. A large cube is made from 27 small cubes. The outside of the large cube is then painted.

Write down the number of small cubes which are

(a) painted on 3 faces   (b) painted on 2 faces

_________   _________

(c) painted on only 1 face   (d) not painted

_________   _________

(e) The outside of a large cube made from 64 small cubes is painted. How many small cubes remain unpainted?

____

25. (a) Which three consecutive numbers, when added together, make 1320 ?

_______________ , _____________ , _____________

(b) Which three consecutive numbers, when multiplied together, make 1320 ?

_____________ , _____________ , _____________

26. A box is in the shape of a cuboid. It is 30 cm long, 24 cm wide and 12 cm high.

(a) How many 1 cm cubes could be fitted into the box?

____

(b) How many toy building bricks of length 5 cm, width 4 cm and height 2 cm could be
   fitted into the box?

____

27.

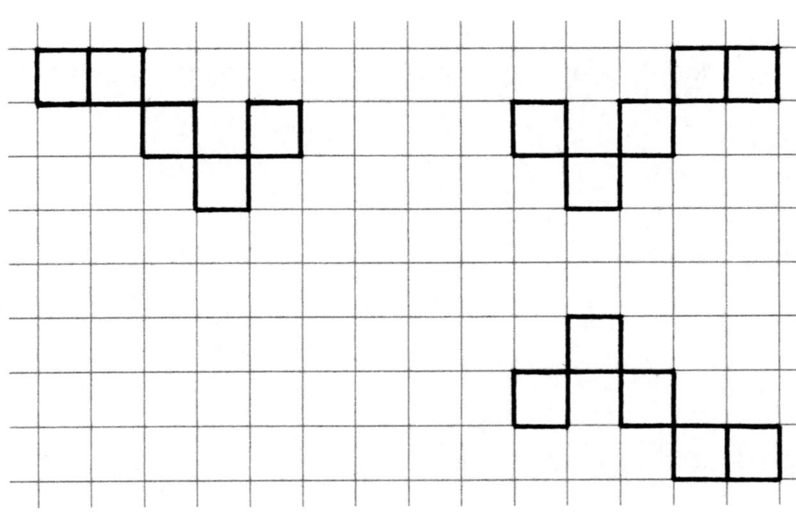

In the diagram, the top two figures are reflections of one another.

The two right-hand figures are reflections of one another.

Draw the two lines of symmetry (mirror lines) which give these reflections.

Draw a fourth figure to make the pattern symmetrical about both lines.

28. If $7N + 1 = 1\,000\,000$, find the value of

(i) $2N$

____

(ii) $3N$

____

(iii) By looking at your answers to (i) and (ii), write down the values of
   $4N$, $5N$ and $6N$.

___________ , ___________ , ___________

29. Brown Rock lighthouse flashes every 18 seconds. Murdoch Head lighthouse flashes every 15 seconds. If they both flash together, how long will it be before they flash together again?

____

30. At Alonso's shop, Maddy bought a fruit pie and three buns. She paid £2.40

Sarah bought 2 fruit pies and 2 buns. She paid £2.80

(a) What was the price of a bun?

____

(b) What was the price of a fruit pie?

____

END OF PAPER A

1.

```
    1 2 3 4
  + 3 5 6 7
  _________
```

____

2. Write the correct numbers above the lines.

(a)   72 ÷ _______ = 9   (b)   111 – _______ = 44

3.   138 × 32

____

4. Subtract seven hundred and nine from one thousand and twenty six.

____

5.

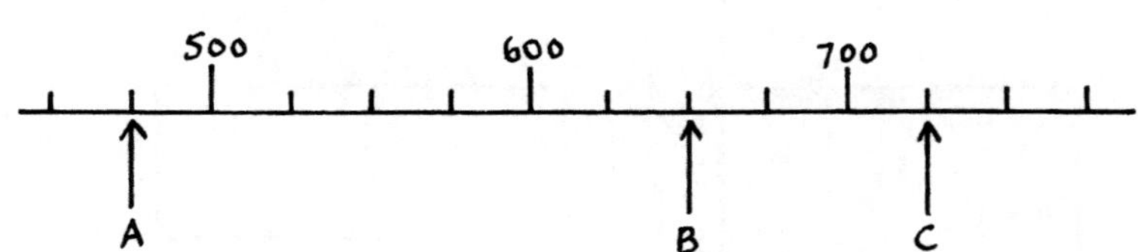

To which numbers do arrows A, B and C point?

A _____________   B _____________   C _____________

6.   (a) $1\frac{3}{4} \times \frac{2}{3}$

____

(b) $1\frac{3}{4} + \frac{2}{3}$

____

7. Add   10·42 , 1·585 and 6

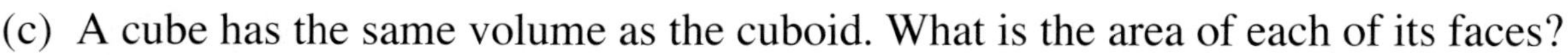

8. A cuboid is 9 inches long, 6 inches wide and 4 inches high.

(a) What is its total surface area?

square inches

(b) What is its volume?

cubic inches

(c) A cube has the same volume as the cuboid. What is the area of each of its faces?

square inches

9. Each of these rectangles (*not drawn to scale*) has the same area. Which has the longest perimeter?

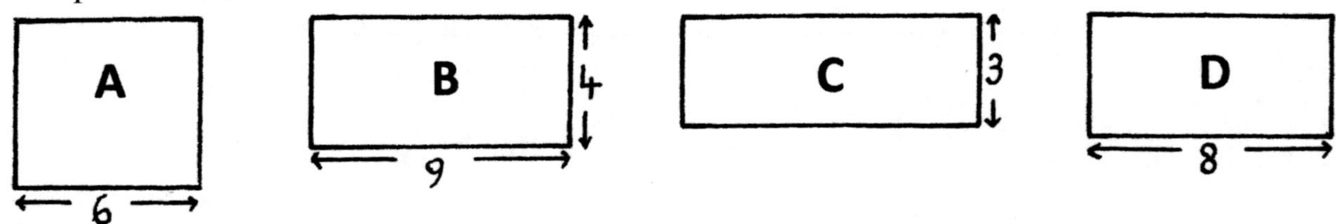

10. Find the next two numbers in each of these sequences.

68 , 61 , 54 , 47 , _______ , _______

400 , 200 , 100 , 50 , _______ , _______

11.

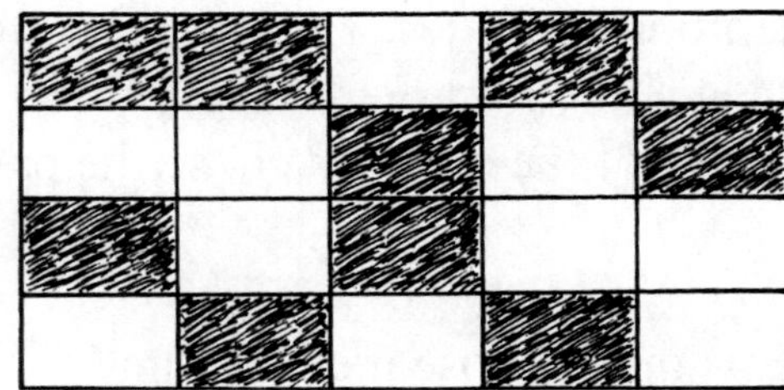

(a) What fraction of the figure is shaded?

____

(b) Express this fraction as a percentage.

____

(c) Express the **un**shaded fraction as a decimal.

____

12. Mr Moss bought 3 newspapers at 75p each, 2 magazines at £1.20 each, and a paperback book at £1.95.

(a) What was the total cost?

____

(b) He paid the exact amount with a £5 note and three coins. Which three coins were they?

____

13. This 'machine' processes a number to give a final answer.

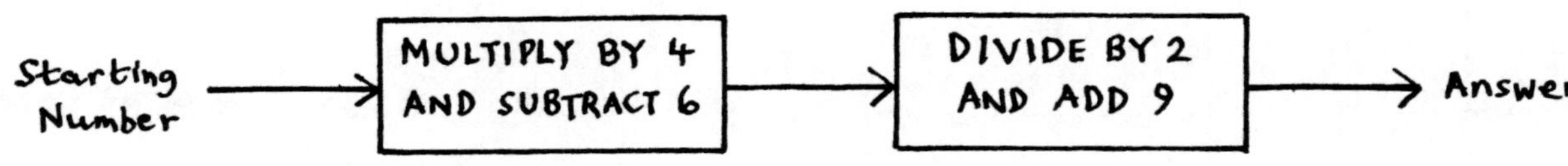

Example: 5 ➔ [× 4 = 20 ; 20 − 6 = 14] ➔ [14 ÷ 2 = 7 ; 7 + 9 =] ➔ 16

(a) What answer is obtained if the starting number is $6\frac{1}{2}$?

____

(b) If the answer is 2, what is the starting number?

____

14.

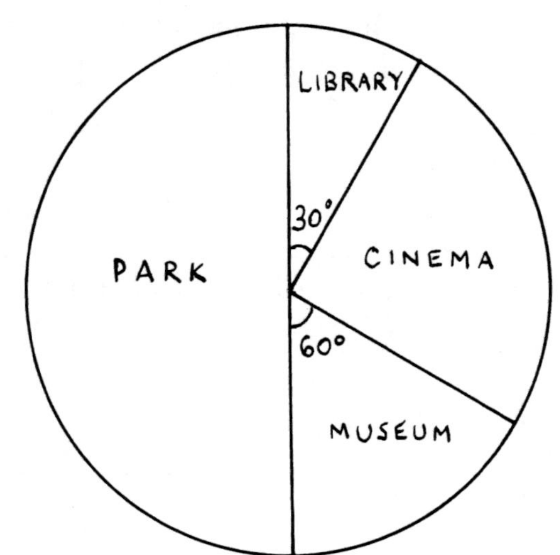

A group of 48 children was given a choice of afternoon activities. They could go to the cinema, the library, the museum or the park. Half of the children chose the park.

(a) How many chose the museum?

____

(b) How many chose the cinema?

____

15. Two numbers add up to 372. One of the numbers is three times the size of the other number.

What is the smaller of the two numbers?

____

16.

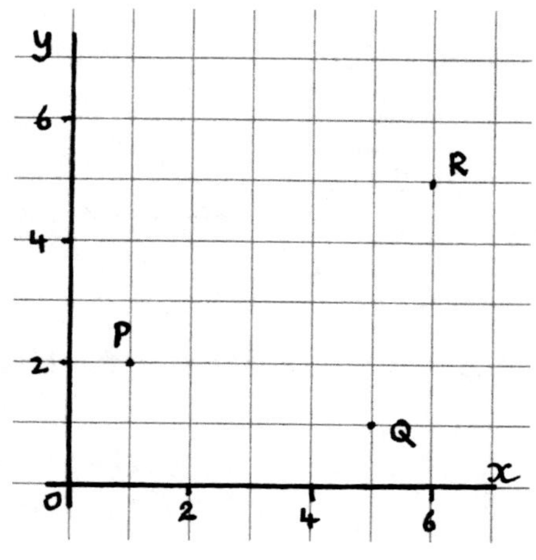

In the diagram, the coordinates of point P are (1 , 2).

(a) Write down the coordinates of point R.

____

(b) Points P, Q, R and S form a square. What are the coordinates of S?

____

(c) What are the coordinates of the centre of the square?

____

17. Write these numbers in order of size, starting with the largest.

$$0{\cdot}070 \ , \ 70{\cdot}00 \ , \ 0{\cdot}770 \ , \ 0{\cdot}007 \ , \ 7{\cdot}000 \ , \ 0{\cdot}707$$

18.

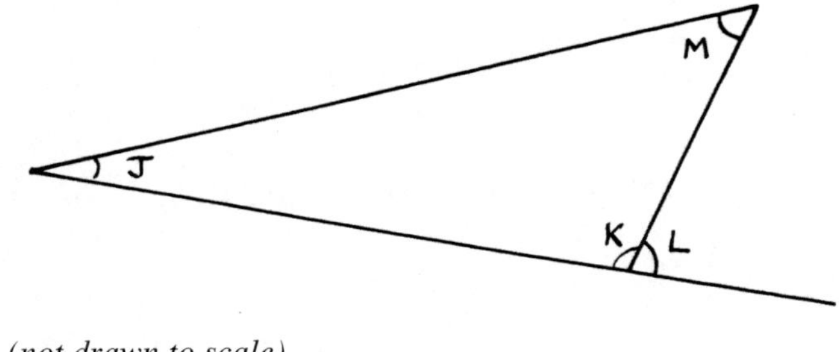

(not drawn to scale)

Angle L = 77°

Angle M = 55°

(a) K is an obtuse angle. What kind of angle is J?

____

(b) Calculate the size of angle K.

____

(c) Calculate the size of angle J.

____

19. A charity is hoping to raise a total of £600 but so far they have raised only 89% of the total. How much more money do they need to reach the total?

____

20. Find the value of w in each of these equations.

(i) $3w + 5 = 17$

____

(ii) $11w = 35 + 6w$

____

(iii) $\dfrac{2w}{3} = 32$

____

21. The timetable shows the times of five trains (A, B, C, D and E) from Idsley to Cottswick.

		A	B	C	D	E
Idsley	_depart_	1544	1618	1644	1714	1738
Winton Wood		1558	1632	1658	1728	1752
Ullenhill		1602	--	--	--	1757
Keeton Green		1609	1641	--	1738	1804
Ackfield		1615	1647	1710	1743	1809
Cottswick	_arrive_	1632	1702	1726	1801	1825

(a) Which is the slowest train to complete the full journey?

____

(b) How long does the fastest train take to make the complete journey?

____

(c) How many trains stop at Ullenhill?

____

(d) Carla lives in Keeton Green. A friend drops her at Idsley station at 1635. How long must she wait there until the next train leaves for Keeton Green?

____

22. The 3rd of March 2003 could be written 03/03/03.
  The 9th of September 2009 could be written 09/09/09.
  The 12th of December 2012 could be written 12/12/12.

On which day of which month of which year will it next be possible to write the date in this way?

____

23. Four boys celebrate their birthdays on the same day each year.
  Douglas is younger than Philip but older than William.
  Philip is 7 years older than Mark who is half William's age.
  Four years from now, Mark will be 9. How old will Douglas be?

____

24.

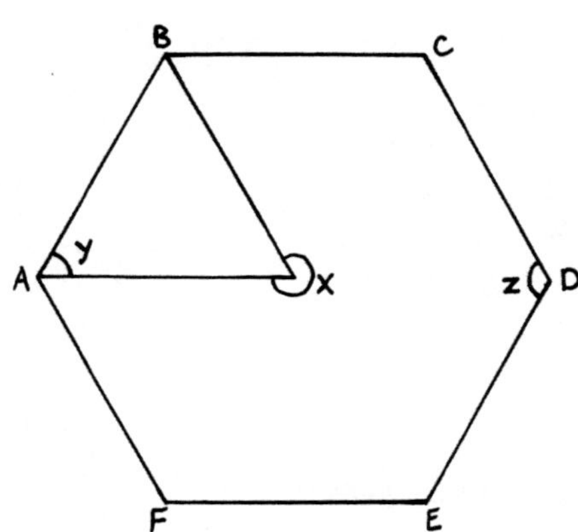

ABCDEF is a polygon with all its sides equal in length.

(i) What kind of polygon is it?

____

Angle x is at the centre of the polygon.

(ii) What is the size of angle x?

____

(iii) What is the size of angle y?

____

(iv) What is the size of angle z?

____

25. A fruit grower plants a straight row of 15 apple trees. The distance between each tree and the next is 3·5 metres. What is the distance from the first tree in the row to the last?

____

26. Fernwood Drive has 41 houses which are numbered with odd numbers on one side (starting at 1) and even numbers on the other side (starting at 2).

Darren's house number is an odd number greater than 3 but smaller than 11. Charlene's house is on the same side of the road and her house number is a multiple of Darren's. What are the possible numbers for Charlene's house?

____

27. Amber's uncle is twice Amber's age; Bella's uncle is three times Bella's age. Amber's and Bella's ages add up to 34. Their uncles' ages add up to 81.

(i) How old is Bella?

____

(ii) How old is Amber's uncle?

____

28. L, M and N stand for three consecutive digits.

(a) In this sum

```
    L M N
    N L M
+   M N L
---------
```

the answer is 1332 .

What are the values of L, M and N?

_______ , _______ and _______

(b) What would the values of L, M and N be to give half the answer in (a)?

_______ , _______ and _______

(c) What would the values of L, M and N be to give twice the answer in (a)?

_______ , _______ and _______

29.

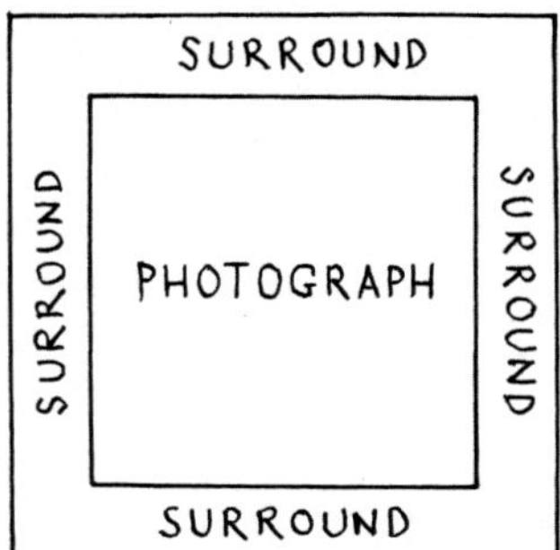

A square photograph 12 cm long is mounted on a square card which is 5 cm longer than the photograph. Which has the larger area, the photograph or the surround, and by how much?

____

30. The height, in centimetres, of a stack of boxes can be shown by the formula

$$H = 7B + 3L$$

where B stands for the number of big boxes and L stands for the number of little boxes.

(i) If B = 4 and L = 9, how high is the stack of boxes?

____

(ii) How many big boxes and how many little boxes are there if the height of the stack is 36 cm?

Number of big boxes

____

Number of little boxes

____

END OF PAPER B

(BLANK PAGE)

1.
$$\begin{array}{r} 1\ 8\ 7\ 6 \\ +\ 3\ 4\ 7\ 7 \\ \hline \end{array}$$

2. Subtract 985 from 6338

3. Find the missing number.

$$11 \quad \times \quad \underline{\hspace{2cm}} \quad = \quad 297$$

4. $2072 \div 8$

5. Write the missing numbers in these sequences.

(a) $\quad 1\frac{1}{2}$, $\underline{\hspace{1.5cm}}$, 6 , 12 , 24 , $\underline{\hspace{1.5cm}}$, 96

(b) $\quad 21$, $17\frac{1}{2}$, 14 , $\underline{\hspace{1.5cm}}$, 7 , $\underline{\hspace{1.5cm}}$, $\underline{\hspace{1.5cm}}$

6. Find the sum of $0{\cdot}868$, 8   and $17{\cdot}05$

7. How many eighths are there in $3\frac{3}{4}$?

8.

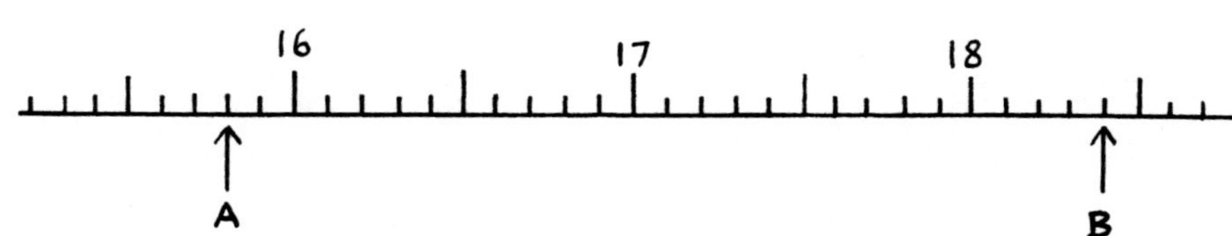

(a) What number is arrow A showing?

____

(b) What number is arrow B showing?

____

(c) What is the average (mean) of these two numbers?

____

9.

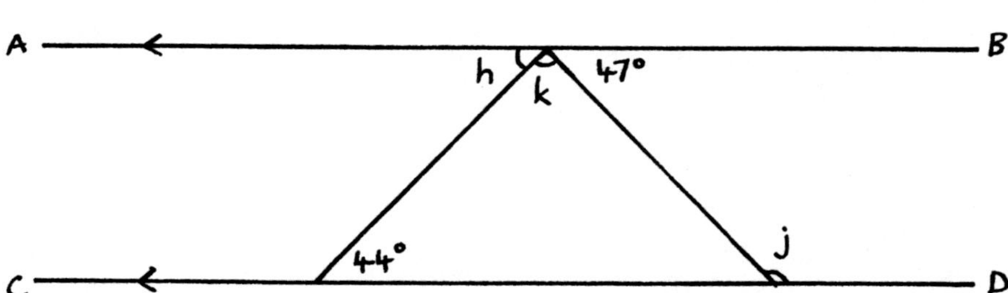

Lines AB and CD are parallel.   *(not drawn to scale)*

Angle h =

____

Angle j   =

____

Angle k =

____

10. (a) Write in figures: thirty million

____

(b) Write in words: 15 050

____

11. Oliver runs twice as fast as Rayyan and three times as fast as Lewis. They all start together and run in the same direction along a straight road. When Oliver has run 150m, how far apart are Rayyan and Lewis?

____

12. If $h = 3$, $j = 4$ and $k = -1$, find the value of

(i) $2j + 5h$

____

(ii) $h + 3k - 4j$

____

(iii) $j^2 \times h$

____

13. The area of a rectangle with sides a and b is 144 cm^2.

(i) What is the perimeter if $b = 4$?

____

(ii) What is the perimeter if $b = 6$?

____

(iii) What is the perimeter if $b = 8$?

____

(iv) What value of b gives the shortest possible perimeter?

____

14. (a) Sam spends £3.23 at a supermarket. He pays with a £5 note. How much change
should he receive?

____

(b) What is the smallest number of coins he could receive?

____

(c) Davina saves 20p coins for a charity. She wants to save £10 altogether but so far has
only £6.40 . How many more 20p coins does she need?

____

15. Fred's Corner Shop sold 72
newspapers of 4 different kinds as shown
in the pie chart.

How many Morning Heralds were sold?

____

16. An airline flight from London to Athens is scheduled to take 3 hours 35 minutes. The
airliner leaves London at 09:55 and arrives in Athens a quarter of an hour late. At what
time does it arrive?

____

17. Jill's birthday is on 28 May. Arisha's birthday is 10 days after Jill's.

(a) On what date is Arisha's birthday? (May has 31 days.)

____

(b) If Arisha's birthday is on a Monday, on which day of the week is Jill's birthday?

____

18.

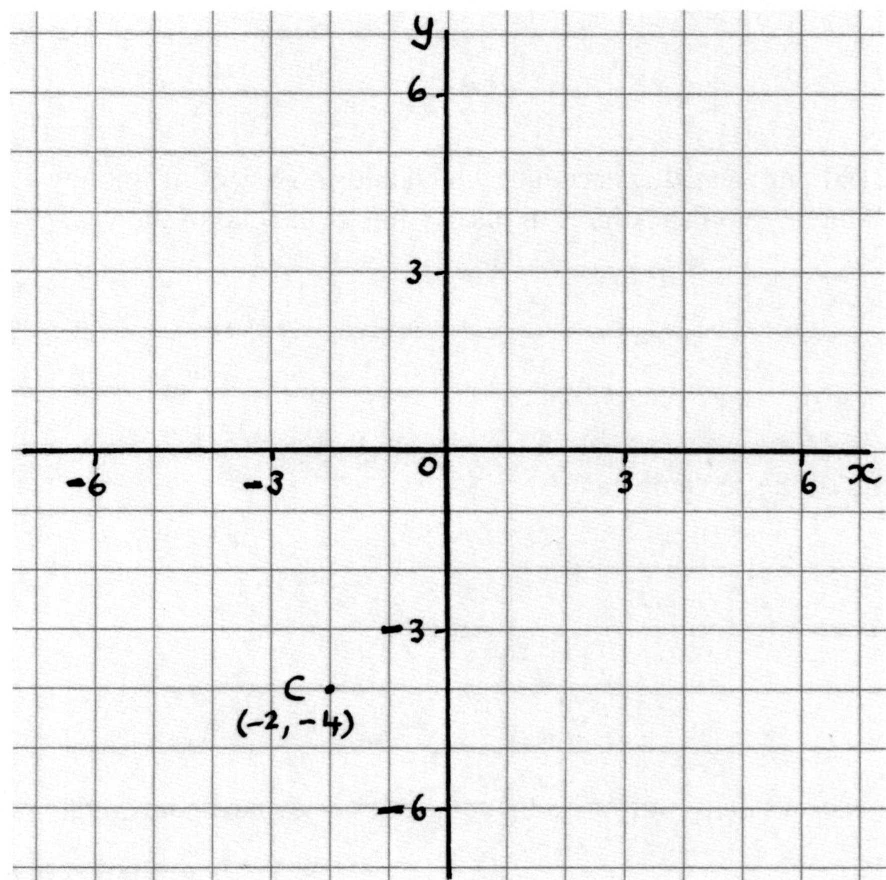

(a) On the grid, plot the points A (1 , 5) and B (4 , 2). Join A, B and C to form a triangle.

(b) Reflect the triangle ABC in the y axis to form triangle JKL.

(c) Join J to A. Join K to B. What shape is ABKJ ?

____

(d) If triangle ABC is extended to form a rectangle ABCD, what are the coordinates of D ?

____

19. A tin full of toffees weighs 470g.
The tin half-full of toffees weighs 295g.
How much does the tin weigh?

____

20. (a) Find 5% of £120

(b) Jack puts £120 into a savings account which adds on 5% of his money at the end of 1 year. How much money will Jack have in his savings at the end of the year?

(c) He then saves the **new** amount of money for another year at 5%. How much money will he have at the end of the second year?

21. The diagram shows the first four terms in a series of squares and stars.

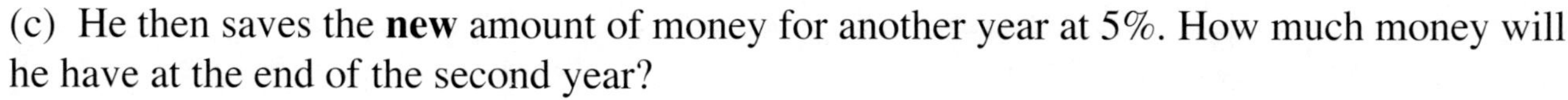

(a) How many squares are there in the seventh term?

(b) How many stars are there in the eighth term?

22.

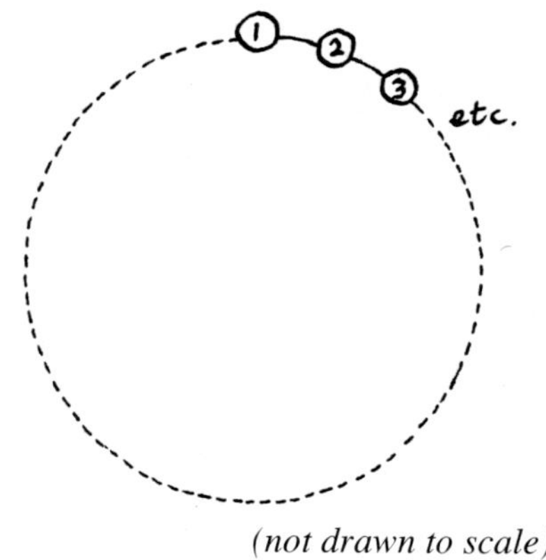

(not drawn to scale)

A group of standing stones (upright megaliths) is arranged symmetrically (evenly spaced) in a circle. When the stones are numbered in order, the fifth stone is directly opposite the twenty-third stone. How many stones are there?

23. (i) I thought of a number, multiplied it by 8 and then added 13. My answer was 61. What number did I first think of?

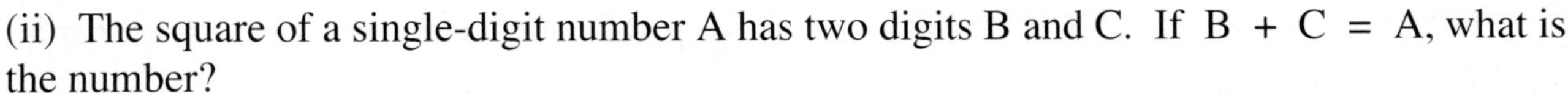

(ii) The square of a single-digit number A has two digits B and C. If B + C = A, what is the number?

____

24. Trains on route A leave Barrington station every $1\frac{1}{2}$ hours. Trains on route B leave Barrington station every $2\frac{1}{2}$ hours. Trains on route A and route B both leave the station together at 7.15 a.m. When will they next leave the station together?

____

25. Leon has £37 ; Abigail has £89 . How much would Abigail have to give Leon for them both to have equal amounts?

____

26. A shop sells 24 phones in five different colours. $\frac{1}{6}$ are black, $\frac{3}{8}$ are blue, $\frac{1}{12}$ are pink and $\frac{1}{4}$ are red. Complete the columns in the graph to show the shop's sales.

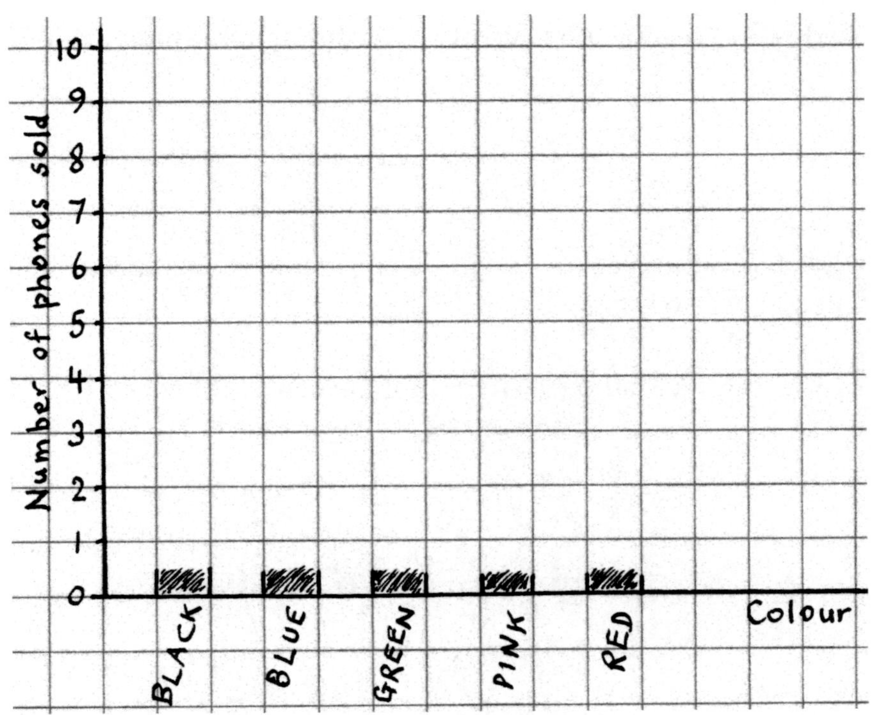

27. There are 15 orange and 10 purple fruit gums in a bag. I take out a gum at random (without looking).

(a) What is the probability that the gum is purple?

____

The gum is purple. I eat it. Then I take out another gum at random.

(b) What is the probability that the gum is **orange**?

____

28. Harry's fish tank is in the shape of a cuboid 40 cm long, 20 cm wide and 30 cm high. He uses a 2 litre jug to pour water into the tank. How many jugfuls of water does he need to fill the tank three-quarters full?

____

29. A map is drawn to a scale of 1 : 2500.

(a) The length of Redland Pond on the map is 94 millimetres. What is its real length in metres?

____

(b) Hawthorn Road is 300 metres long. What is its length, in millimetres, on the map?

____

30. A certain radioactive substance has a half-life of 6 hours. This means that its radioactivity is halved every 6 hours.

What percentage of its original radioactivity will it have after 24 hours?

____

END OF PAPER C

Paper **D**

1. $37 + 4418 + 596$

____

2. $2124 - 786$

____

3. Multiply three thousand six hundred and seventy four by nine. Give your answer in words.

____

4. Find the missing number.

_________ × 7 = 3689

____

5. What is $\frac{3}{4}$ of 18 ?

____

6. (a) Fill in the missing numbers in this sequence. The same number is added to each term to make the next term.

3 , _________ , _________ , _________ , 19

(b) Fill in the missing numbers in this sequence. Each term is divided by the same number to make the next term.

240 , _________ , _________ , _________ , 15

7. If these are written in order of size, which is in the middle?

0·3 , 0·033 , 3·0 , 0·00333 , 0·33

8. (i) What fraction is shaded in each of these squares?

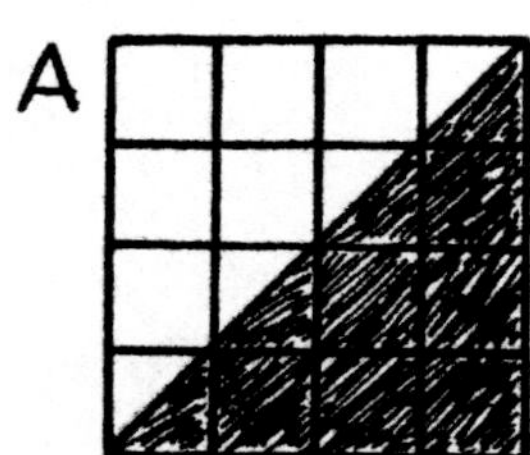  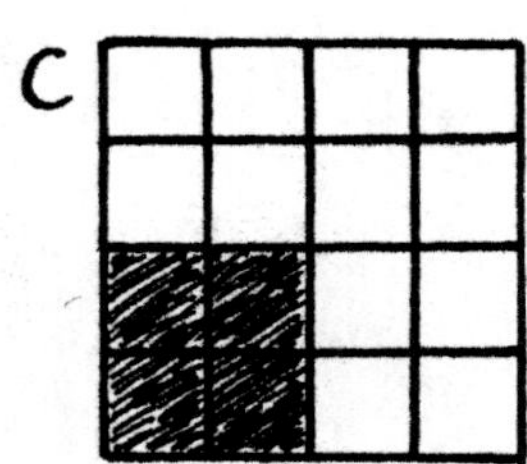

A ________

B ________

C ________

(ii) Find the sum of the three fractions (A + B + C).

____

9. Mrs Jackman's tea urn holds 12 litres of tea. She can fill 25 identical teapots from a full urn. What volume, in millilitres, does each teapot hold?

____

10. Hannah buys 3 frozen meals at £1.65 each, 2 bread loaves at 96p each and 4 oranges at 38p each. She pays with a £10 note. How much change should she receive?

____

11. If x = 5, y = 4, what is the value of each of these expressions?

(i) $2x - 3y$

____

(ii) xy

____

(iii) $3y^2$

____

(iv) $\sqrt{x + y}$

____

12. This shape (not drawn to scale) is made up of two rectangles connected by a square.

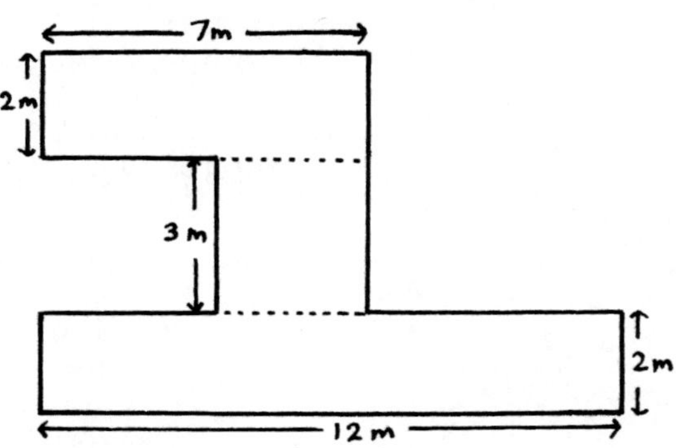

Calculate (a) the area of the shape.

____

(b) the perimeter of the shape.

____

13.

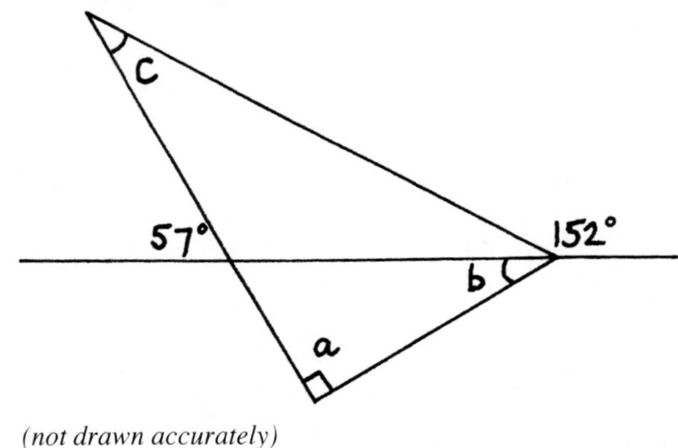

(not drawn accurately)

Angle *a* is a right angle.

Calculate the sizes of angles b and c.

b =

____

c =

____

14. (a) Julie thought of a number. She multiplied it by 3, then subtracted 5 and then divided by 2. The result was 8. What number did she first think of?

____

(b) If, instead, the result had been $-1\frac{3}{4}$, what number would she have first thought of?

____

15.

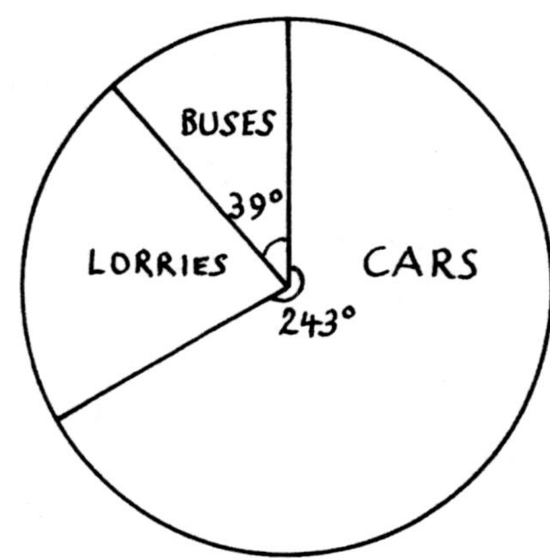

(not drawn accurately)

Giles and Usman counted the traffic (the number of vehicles) going south along a motorway. They made a pie chart to show the results.

They counted 240 vehicles altogether. How many lorries did they count?

____

16. Tamara wants to put 1 Crummy biscuit and 1 Rocky biscuit in her lunch box each day.
Crummy biscuits are sold in packets of 8 ; Rocky biscuits are sold in packets of 12.
She buys the least possible number of packets of biscuits so that no biscuits are left over.

How many packets of Crummy biscuits does she buy?

____

17.

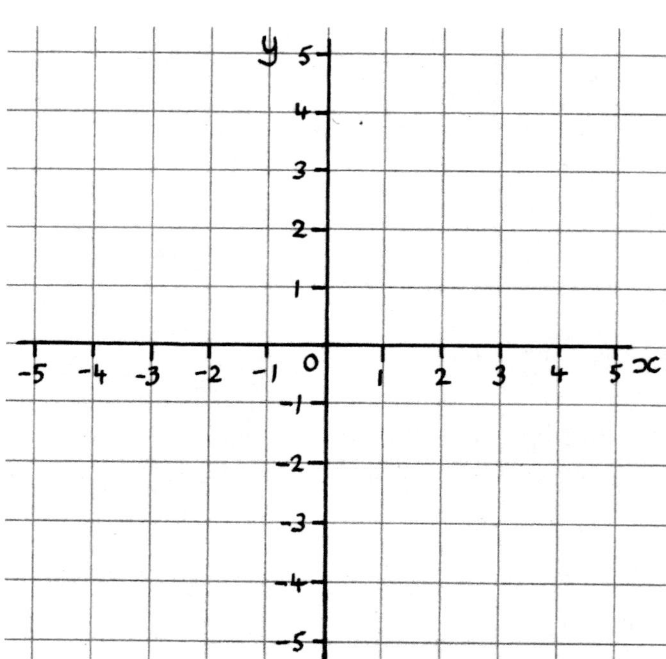

(i) On the grid, plot the graph points A (3 , 1), B (1 , 4) and C (−2 , 2).

(ii) Join these points to form a triangle.

(iii) Reflect triangle ABC in the x axis.

(iv) Plot point D (0 , −1). What shape is ABCD ?

____

page 34

18. Each row, each column and each diagonal adds up to 33. Which number should go in
the square marked x ?

	x	
	11	15
12		

____

19. From this set of numbers

$$42 \ , \ 45 \ , \ 37 \ , \ 47 \ , \ 45 \ , \ 44 \ , \ 41$$

find (a) the mode.

____

(b) the median.

____

(c) the mean (average).

____

(d) the range.

____

20. Look at this four-digit number

6 2 3 8

(a) By rearranging the digits, what is the smallest number that can be made?

____

(b) What is the largest **odd** number that can be made?

____

(c) If the answer to (a) is subtracted from the answer to (b), what is the result to the nearest
hundred?

____

21.

 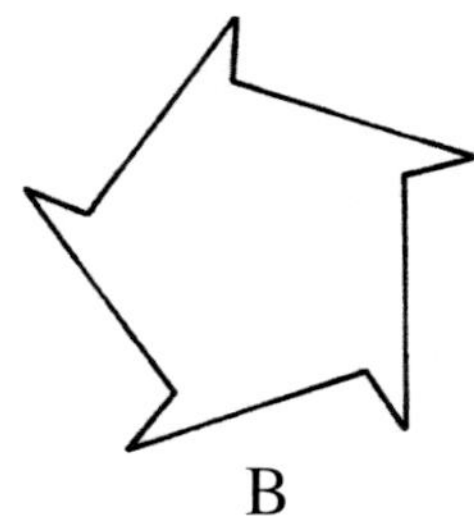 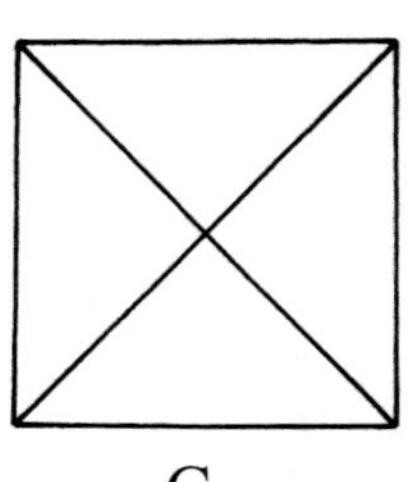 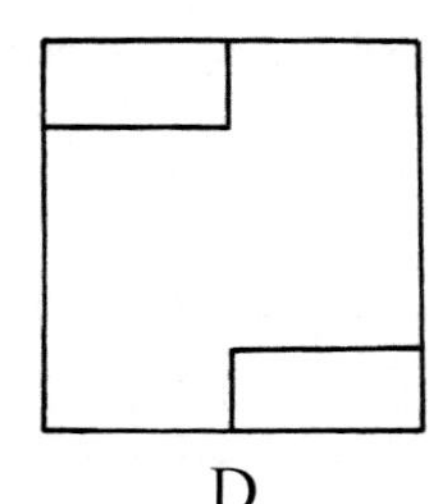

A   B   C   D

(i) Which of the figures have line symmetry?

____

(ii) Which of the figures have rotational symmetry?

____

22. (a)   97 × 46

____

From your answer to (a), work out

(b) 0·97 × 0·46

____

(c) 97 × 23

____

(d) 98 × 23

____

23.

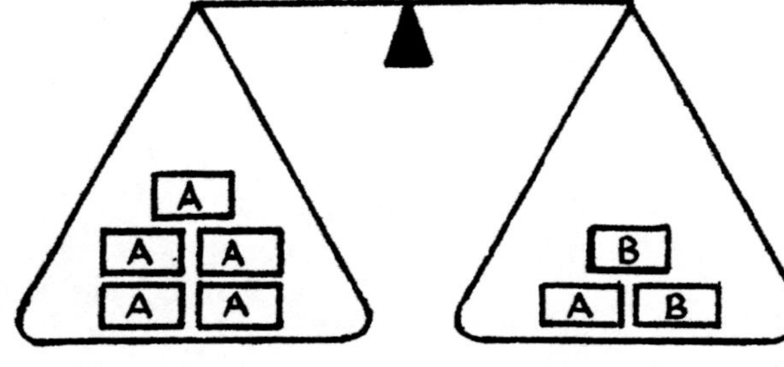 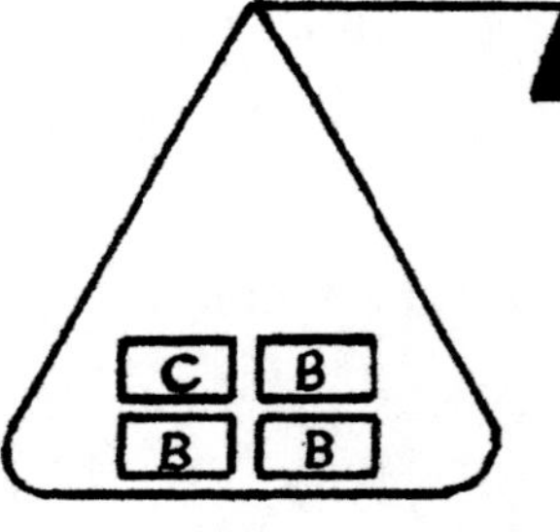 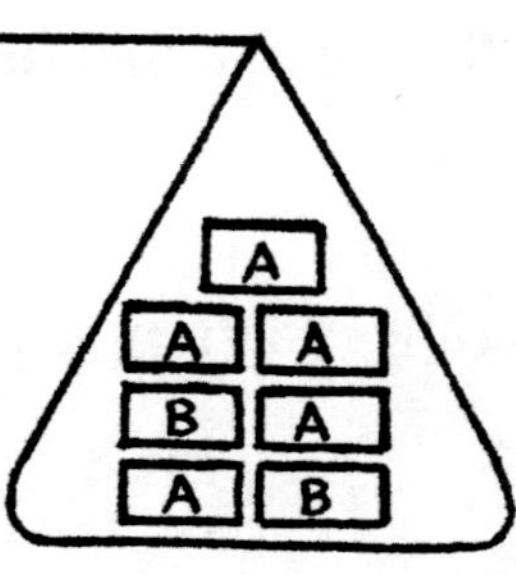

The two balances in the diagram contain blocks of different materials A, B and C.

Each block of material A weighs 95 g.

How much does the block of material C weigh?

____

24. Natasha buys a diamond ring at an auction. The price of the ring (called the hammer price) is £550. The auctioneer then adds a selling fee of 8%.

(a) What is the total cost of the ring with the selling fee added?

____

(b) Natasha must then pay tax which is 20% of the total cost. How much does she pay altogether, including the tax?

____

25. There are 4 bells, each making a different musical note (C, B, A and G). The bells can be rung in any order (Example. BGAC or ABCG). In how many different ways can the bells be rung?

____

26. The Venn diagram represents a group of boys.

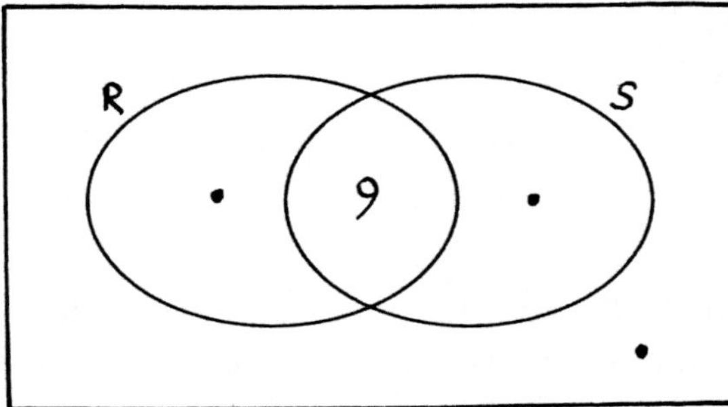

The oval marked R represents boys who play rugby ; the one marked S represents those who play soccer.

One third of the rugby players also play soccer; one quarter of the soccer players also play rugby. 9 play both ; 10 do not play either rugby or soccer.

(a) Complete the diagram by writing the correct number in each space marked with a dot.

(b) How many boys are there in the group?

____

27. If the moon rises at 19:43 hours and sets 9 hours 20 minutes later, at what time does it set?

28. Behind Luke's house there are two piles of bricks. One pile has 95 bricks; the other has 47 bricks. How many bricks must Luke move to make the piles equal?

29.

To make a sculpture, a block of stone in the shape of a thin cuboid 50 cm high and 30 cm wide has a hole cut in the shape of a right-angled isosceles triangle with its equal sides 20 cm long.

The block is 10 cm thick. What is the volume of stone in the finished sculpture?

30. The Jones family have a rectangular garden with perimeter 40m. They buy more land and enlarge the garden, still in the shape of a rectangle, so that it is twice the width and three times the length of the original. The perimeter of the enlarged garden is 104m.

What were the dimensions of the original garden?

Length   Width

END OF PAPER D

1. 426 + 117 + 265

____

2. 8107 ÷ 11

____

3. 165 × 33

____

4. What must be added to 7 to make 7 squared?

____

5. (a) Three cream cakes are shared equally between four people. What fraction of a cake does each person have?

____

    (b) How many fifths are there in five?

____

6. Find the sum of   6·32 , 0·5 , 4 and 0·07

____

7. Write in figures: one million forty three thousand and ninety two.

____

8. (a) Subtract 1234 from 4321.

$\underline{\hspace{5cm}}$

(b) Subtract 2345 from 5432.

$\underline{\hspace{5cm}}$

(c) Without doing any working, write down the answer to 9876 − 6789.

$\underline{\hspace{5cm}}$

9.

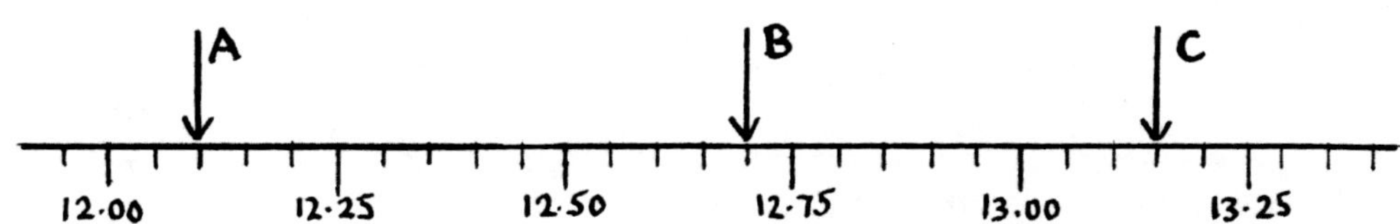

(i) What amounts do arrows A, B and C point to?

A $\underline{\hspace{3cm}}$ B $\underline{\hspace{3cm}}$ C $\underline{\hspace{3cm}}$

(ii) Calculate the difference between B and C.

$\underline{\hspace{5cm}}$

10. Find the next two numbers in each sequence.

(a) 128 , 64 , 32 , $\underline{\hspace{2cm}}$, $\underline{\hspace{2cm}}$

(b) 14 , 17 , 21 , 24 , 28 , 31 , $\underline{\hspace{2cm}}$, $\underline{\hspace{2cm}}$

11.

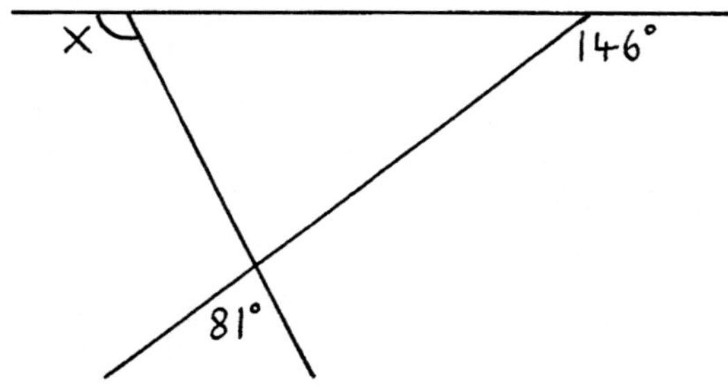

Calculate the size of angle x.

$\underline{\hspace{5cm}}$

page 40

12. The school day at Blakemore School starts at 8.50 a.m. and ends at 3.15 p.m.

(a) How long is the school day?

_________ h _________ min

(b) How would the starting and ending times be written in 24-hour clock?

Start _____________ End _____________

13.

(a) What fraction of the square is NOT black?

____

(b) The square has one line of symmetry.

Draw the line of symmetry on the square.

14. One winter day the temperature at 5.00 a.m. was $-8 \cdot 0°$ C. At 9.00 a.m. it was $-1 \cdot 5°$ C and at 2.00 p.m. it was $10 \cdot 0°$ C.

(a) How much did the temperature rise between 5.00 a.m. and 9.00 a.m. ?

____

(b) What was the hourly average (mean) rate of temperature rise between 5.00 a.m. and 2.00 p.m. ?

____

15. An adult day ticket to Greenberry Theme Park is £9.50. A child's ticket costs $\frac{3}{5}$ of an adult ticket.

Mr and Mrs Bland spend a day at the park with their three children.

They pay with two £20 notes. How much change should they receive?

____

16.

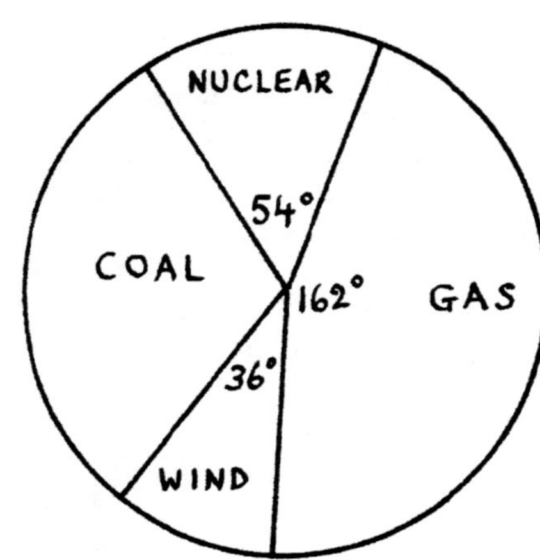

The power stations in a certain country are fuelled by gas, coal, wind or nuclear energy. The pie chart shows the proportion of power stations using the different fuels.

What **percentage** of power stations are fuelled by coal ?

---

17. One inch is roughly equal to 25 millimetres.   1 foot = 12 inches.

(a) Uncle Archie's car is 14 feet long. What, roughly, is its length in millimetres?

(b) The car is 1800 millimetres wide. What, roughly, is its width in feet?

---

18. Fill in the squares to make these correct.

Addition

$$
\begin{array}{r}
4\ 7\ \square \\
6\ 8 \\
+\quad 9\ \square\ 1 \\
\hline
1\ \square\ 6\ 2
\end{array}
$$

Division

$$
5\ )\ \overline{\ \square\ 8\ 5\ }\quad 9\ \square
$$

19. Write down the value of

(a) the square of 18

(b) 5 cubed

(c) the square root of 144

(d) the cube root of −27

20. Solve these equations

    (i) $3t - 5 = 16$

$$t = \underline{\hspace{3cm}}$$

    (ii) $\dfrac{w}{3} + 3 = 11$

$$w = \underline{\hspace{3cm}}$$

21.

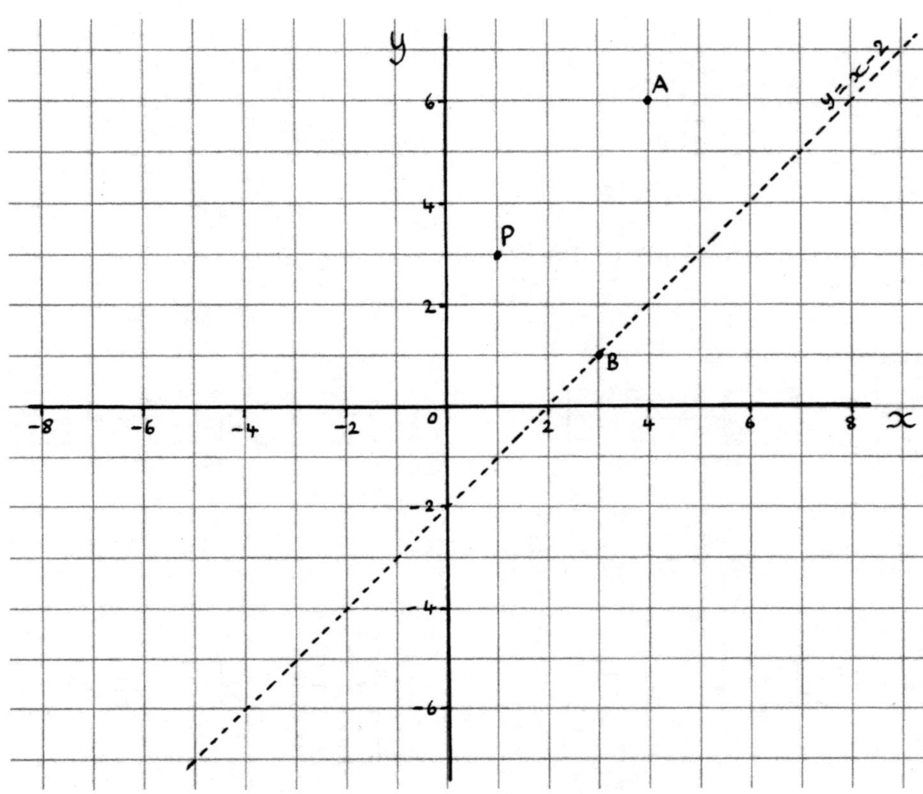

Point P (1 , 3) is the centre of a rhombus.   Points A (4 , 6) and B (3 , 1) are corners of the rhombus.

(i) Find the other two corners and draw the complete rhombus.

(ii) Write down the coordinates of the two other corners.

$$\underline{\hspace{4cm}} \; , \; \underline{\hspace{4cm}}$$

(iii) Reflect the rhombus in the dotted line (y=x–2) to form a new rhombus.

(iv) Write down the coordinates of the centre of the new rhombus.

$$\underline{\hspace{4cm}}$$

22.

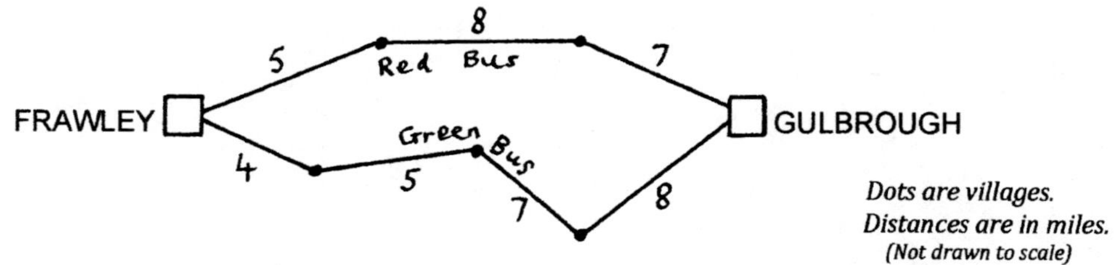

The diagram shows two different bus routes between Frawley and Gulbrough. The red bus travels at 15 miles/hour (m.p.h) ; the green bus travels at 20 miles/hour.

Both buses set off from Frawley at the same time. Which bus takes the shorter time to reach Gulbrough, and by how many minutes?

________________ bus by ___________ minutes

23. This machine processes numbers in a certain way.

Examples.

Using the machine, find the values of F, G and H ?

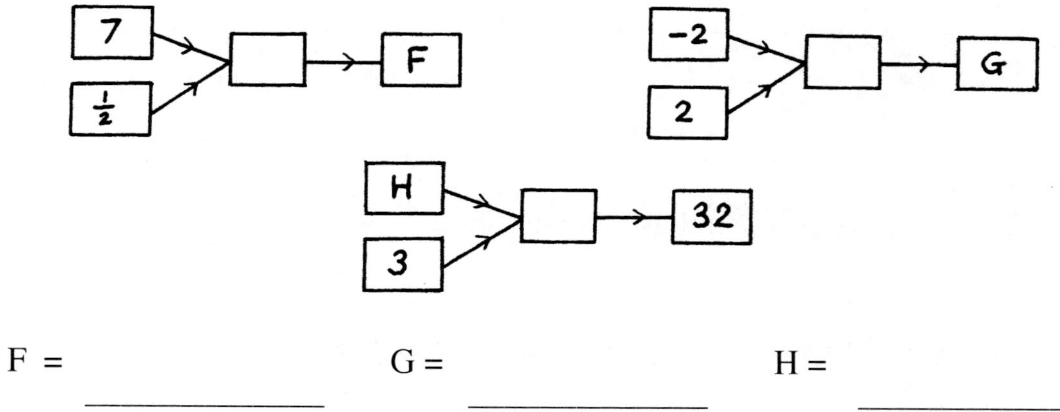

F = ___________   G = ___________   H = ___________

24. A radio-controlled mouse starts at an oak tree and goes 7 m east, then 9 m south, then 11 m west, then 3 m north, then 4 m east.

How far is the mouse from the oak tree?

____

25. (a) Kaylah was born after the year 2003 and before 2017. The year of her birth does not divide equally by 2, 3, 5 or 7. In which year was she born?

____

(b) The month she was born has only 30 days, and a name of 4 letters. In which month was she born?

____

(c) The day of the month she was born is the highest possible prime number. On which day of the month was she born?

____

26. Brenda spent five days training for a long-distance walk. Each day she walked three miles further than the previous day. By the end of the fifth day she had walked 125 miles.

How far did she walk on the second day?

____

27.

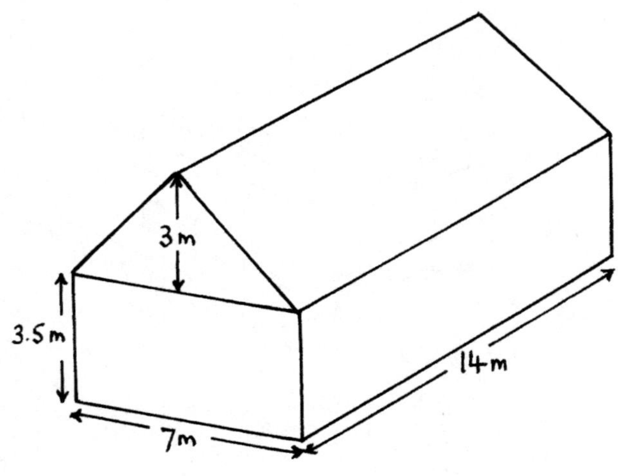

The drawing represents a house 14m long, 7m wide and 6·5m high. The end wall of the house is in the shape of a rectangle surmounted by an isosceles triangle.

Calculate the total inside space (the volume) of the house.

____

28. A pile of 40 similar boxes is 2·2 metres high.   What is the height, in millimetres, of each box ?

____

29. In Roman numbers **I** means 1 ;   **V** means 5 ;   **X** means 10 .

L = V times X ;   **C** = X times X ;   **D** = V times C ;   **M** = X times C .

To make an amount, the letters are added, e.g. XXVII means 27, DLXXXV means 585, etc.

(a) What does the Roman number MDCXVIII mean?

____

(b) How is 2371 written as a Roman number?

____

30. Each layer in this stepped pyramid has half the volume of the layer directly beneath it.

The top layer has a volume of 3 cm^3.
What is the volume of the complete pyramid?

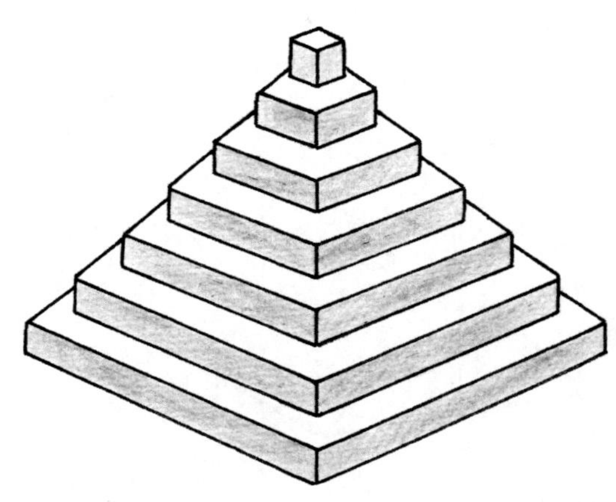

____

END OF PAPER E

1.

$$\begin{array}{r} 4\ 1\ 6\ 2 \\ -\ \ \ 8\ 3\ 7 \\ \hline \end{array}$$

____

2.

$$\begin{array}{r} 6\ 2\ 5\ 8 \\ \times\ \ \ \ \ \ \ 7 \\ \hline \end{array}$$

____

3. A, B and C are three different digits. Copy this sum, replacing letters A, B and C with the correct numbers.

$$\begin{array}{r} 2\ \ A\ \ A\ \ 2 \\ +\ \ 5\ \ B\ \ B\ \ 5 \\ \hline B\ \ C\ \ 5\ \ A \end{array} \qquad \begin{array}{r} 2\ \ \ \ \ \ \ \ \ 2 \\ +\ \ 5\ \ \ \ \ \ \ \ 5 \\ \hline 5 \end{array}$$

4. Divide 9138 by 6.

____

5. Write down all the ten prime numbers which are less than 30.

______ , ______ , ______ , ______ , ______ , ______ , ______ , ______ , ______ , ______

6. Write the correct numbers in the empty boxes.

(i) $43\ +\ \boxed{}\ =\ 101$

(ii) $\boxed{}\ \times\ 500\ =\ 20\,000$

(iii) $15\ -\ \boxed{}\ =\ 6\frac{1}{2}$

7.

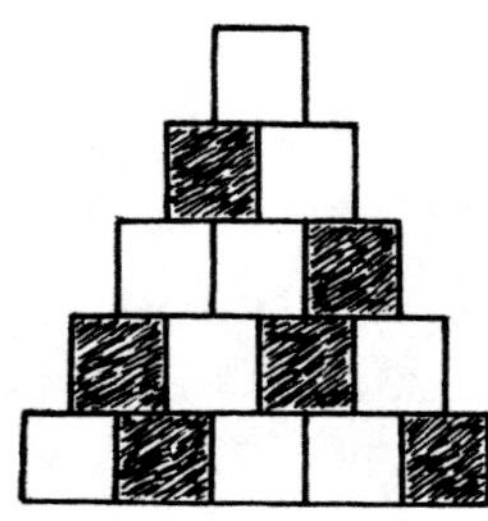

(b) Express the fraction as a decimal.

____

(a) What fraction of the shape is shaded?

(c) Express the UNSHADED fraction as a percentage.

____

____

8. Simplify

   (a) $2\frac{5}{6} - 1\frac{1}{4}$

____

   (b) $3\frac{1}{5} \times \frac{3}{4} \times 1\frac{7}{8}$

____

   (c) $\frac{5}{8} \div \frac{15}{16}$

____

9. In one week, the level of water in a river rises from 85 cm to 218 cm.

What is the average (mean) daily rise in level?

____

10. A shop sold 29 roast chickens at £5.25 each. How much money did the shop receive?

____

11.

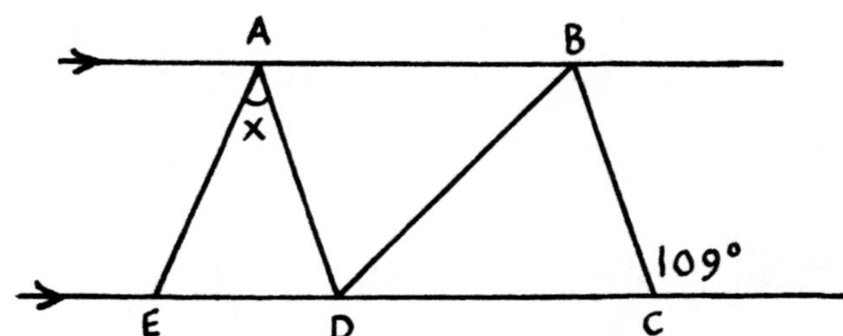

ABCDE is an isosceles trapezium made from three isosceles triangles (*not drawn to scale*).
AB = BD = CD and AD = AE. AB and EC are parallel.

(a) What kind of quadrilateral is ABCD?

____

(b) What kind of quadrilateral is ABDE?

____

(c) What size is angle x ?

____

12.

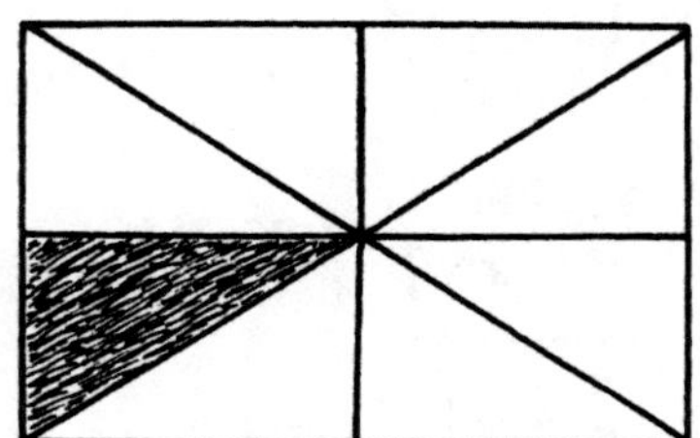

In this rectangle (*not drawn to scale*) the shaded triangle has an area of 26 cm². The longer side of the rectangle has a length of 16 cm.

Calculate the perimeter of the rectangle.

____

13. (a) Fill in the missing numbers in this sequence. The same number is subtracted from each term to make the next term.

37 , _________ , _________ , _________ , 13

(b) Fill in the missing numbers in this sequence. Each term is multiplied by the same number to make the next term.

$\dfrac{1}{3}$, _________ , _________ , _________ , 27

14. Martha wants to cover a rectangular floor with square tiles of length 30 cm. The floor measures 5·4 m by 4·5 m.

How many tiles will she need?

____

15. If a = 3 , b = 2 , find the values of

(i)   3a + 5b

____

(ii) a² ÷ b

____

(iii) 5ab – 7

____

16.

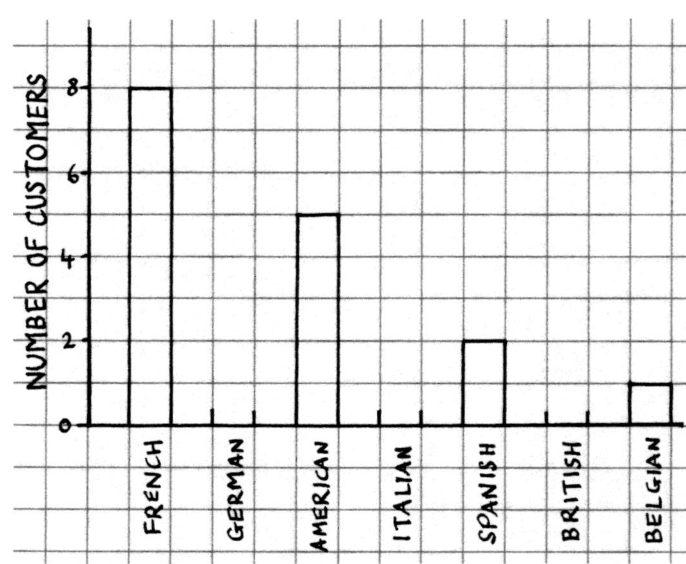

The nationalities of the first 30 customers on a certain day at the Café Mondrianne are shown on the unfinished graph. One sixth of the customers were British. There were twice as many Italians as Germans.

Draw the missing three columns to complete the graph.

17. What is the angle between the hands of a clock when the time is

(a) two o'clock?

____

(b) half past six?

____

(c) twenty (minutes) past eight?

____

18. A train leaves Darwin on Wednesday at 10.00 a.m. and arrives in Katherine at 1.40 p.m.

(a) How long does the journey take?

_______ h   _______ min

(b) After 4 hours 40 minutes in Katherine, the train sets off again, arriving in Alice Springs at 9.10 a.m. on Thursday.

How long does the journey take from Katherine to Alice Springs?

_______ h   _______ min

19.

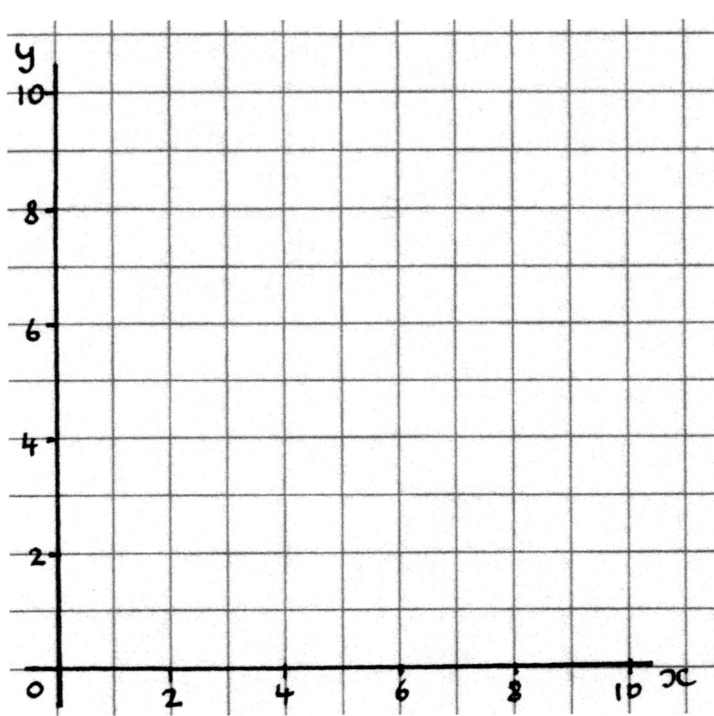

Plot A with coordinates (6 , 5); plot B with coordinates (8 , 9).

A is the centre of a square; B is one corner of the square.

(i) Draw the complete square.

(ii) Draw a larger square with corners (2 , 1), (2 , 9), (10 , 9) and (10 , 1). By finding the area of the larger square, or by any other method, calculate the area of the original square in square units. (The length of each red square is 1 unit.)

____

20. Find the value of

[a] 8 × 2 – 15 ÷ 3

____

[b] 5 + (7 – 1) × 2

____

[c] 6 – 24 ÷ 4

____

[d] 11 + 3 × 9 – (2 + 3)

____

21.

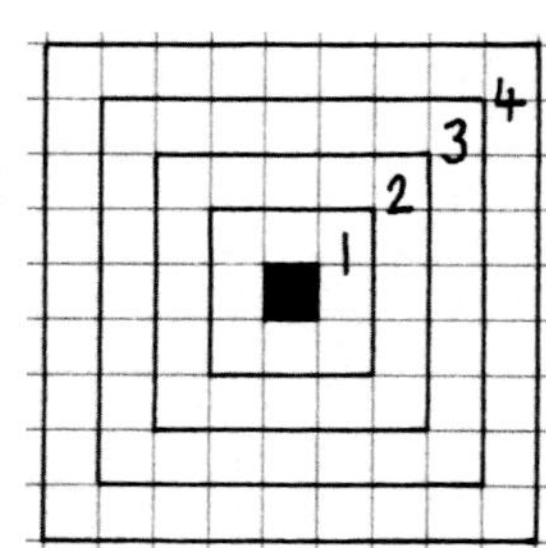

The small, black square is surrounded by 'shells' of larger squares. The first four shells are shown in the diagram. There are eight small squares in the first shell.

How many small squares are there in the fifty-first shell?

____

22. 2! is called '2 factorial'. It means 2 × 1
3! is called '3 factorial'. It means 3 × 2 × 1
4! = 4 × 3 × 2 × 1,   etc.

Work out the values of

(a) 6!

____

(b) 7!

____

(c) 7! ÷ 6!

(d) Without calculating 19! and 20!, write down the value of 20! ÷ 19!

____

23.

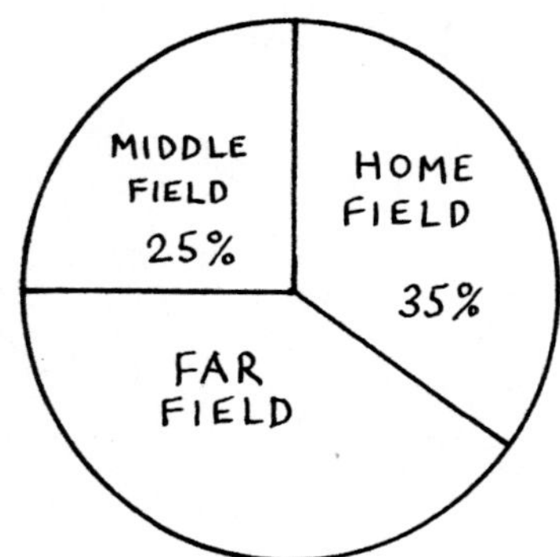

Farmer Wilson has a flock of sheep which
are grazing in three different fields as
shown by the pie chart.

(a) What percentage of his sheep are in
the Far Field?

____

(b) There are 64 sheep in the Far Field.
How many sheep are there altogether?

____

24. Dad weighs (has a mass of) 90 kg. The weights (masses) of his four children are

        Rob : one half of Dad's
        Lara : one third of Dad's
        Freddie : one fifth of Dad's
        Kate : three tenths of Dad's

What is the total weight of the children?

____

25. A box contains 6 white tennis balls and 4 yellow tennis balls.

(a) If I choose a ball without looking, what is the probability that it will be yellow?

____

(b) I keep the yellow ball and choose another ball from the box. What is the probability that
it will be yellow?

____

26. Duncan's water tank is already one quarter full. He puts another 825 litres of water into the tank. It is now seven eighths full. How much water does the tank hold?

27. On platform 3 there were 68 people waiting for a train.

36 wore glasses ; 29 wore a hat ; 20 wore neither glasses nor a hat.

(a) How many wore both a hat and glasses?

(b) How many wore a hat but did not wear glasses?

28.

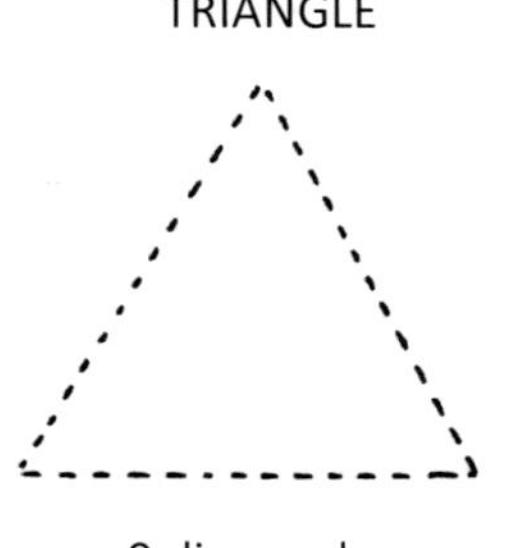

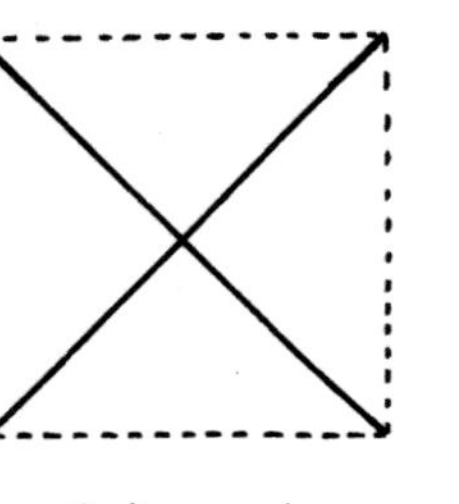

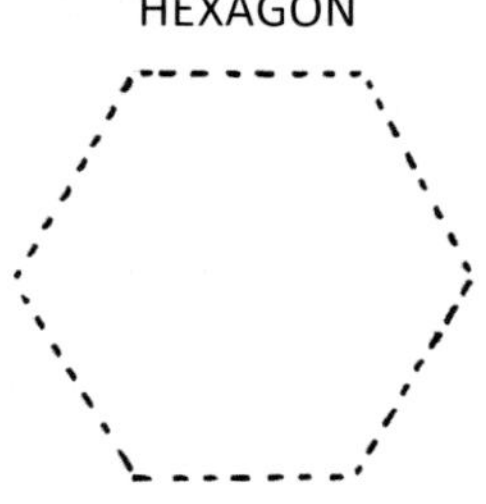

(a) How many diagonals has a HEXAGON ?

The formula for the number of diagonals in an x-sided figure is $\dfrac{x(x-3)}{2}$.

(b) How many diagonals has a ICOSAGON (20-sided figure)?

(c) A certain polygon has 35 diagonals. How many sides has it?

29. Mr Jarville is constructing a brick wall. Each brick is 75 mm high. How many layers of bricks will he need to make the wall at least 1 metre high?

____

30. My bicycle combination lock has a four-digit code number (a number between 0000 and 9999 inclusive).

The number on my lock is prime, and its digits are consecutive. What is the number?

____

END OF PAPER F

(BLANK PAGE)

1.
$$\begin{array}{r} 2\ 5\ 9\ 2 \\ +\ \ \ 7\ 4\ 1 \\ \hline \end{array}$$

2.
$$\begin{array}{r} 5\ 2\ 0\ 9 \\ -\ 4\ 3\ 2\ 1 \\ \hline \end{array}$$

3. Multiply: 576 × 6

4. Divide: 3108 ÷ 7

5. Write in figures: sixty thousand and seventy.

6. Write down the amounts shown by arrows P, Q and R.

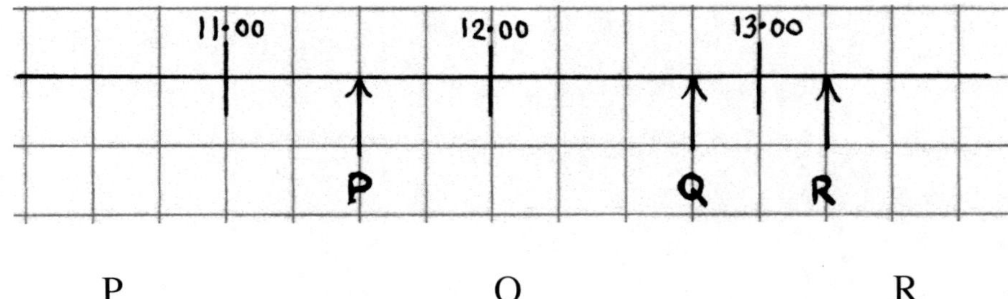

P   Q   R

7. Complete each square by writing the correct sign (+ , − , × , ÷).

(a) 8 ☐ 3 ☐ 5   = 29

(b)   54 ☐ 2 = 30 ☐ 3

8. Simplify

(a) $\dfrac{90}{225}$

____

(b) $\dfrac{1}{2} + \dfrac{2}{3} - \dfrac{3}{4}$

____

9. Find the cost of 36 bicycles at £125 each.

____

10. Add together 0·009 , 9 , 0·9 , 0·99 and 90

____

11.

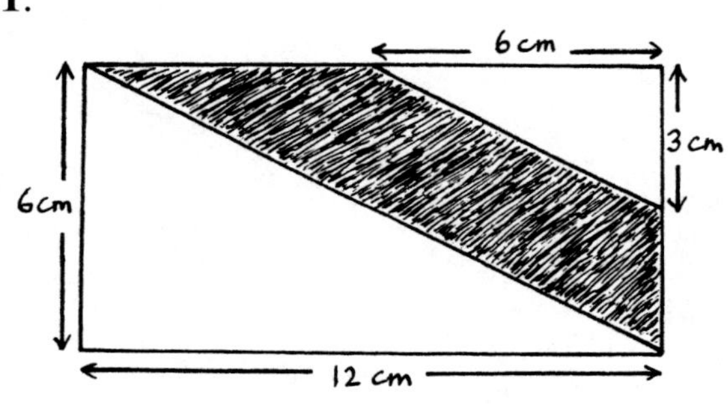

(a) Calculate the perimeter of the rectangle (_not drawn accurately_).

____

(b) Calculate the area of the shaded part.

____

12. Write these amounts in order of size, starting with the largest.

$$\dfrac{7}{8} \ , \quad 0\cdot8 \ , \quad 86\% \ , \quad \dfrac{6}{7} \ , \quad 0\cdot88$$

____

13.

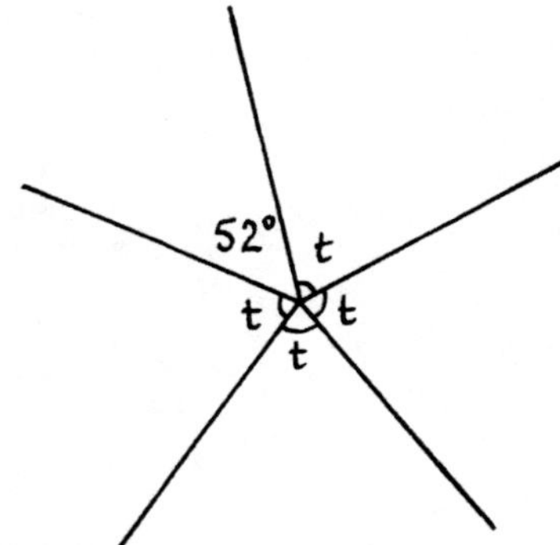

(not drawn accurately)

What is the value of t ?

____

14. The length, width and height of a (cuboid) box are in the ratio 4 : 2 : 1. Its height is 1 cm.

(a) Calculate the volume of the box.

____

(b) A similar box has a height of 3 cm. Calculate its volume.

____

(c) What is the ratio of the volume of the small box to the volume of the large box ?

____

15. Alice bought 2 packs of tomatoes at 76p a pack, a cauliflower at 96p, 2 packs of mushrooms at 87p a pack and a cucumber at £1.25 . She paid with three £2 coins. How much change did she receive?

____

16.

		2
1	**5**	

Each vertical, horizontal and diagonal in this square has a total of 15.

Complete the square with the correct numbers.

17. (i) d + d =

____

(ii) d − d =

____

(iii) d × d =

____

(iv) d ÷ d =

____

(v) If $d = 7\frac{3}{4}$, what is the value of d + d ?

____

(vi) If d = −3 , what is the value of d × d ?

____

18.

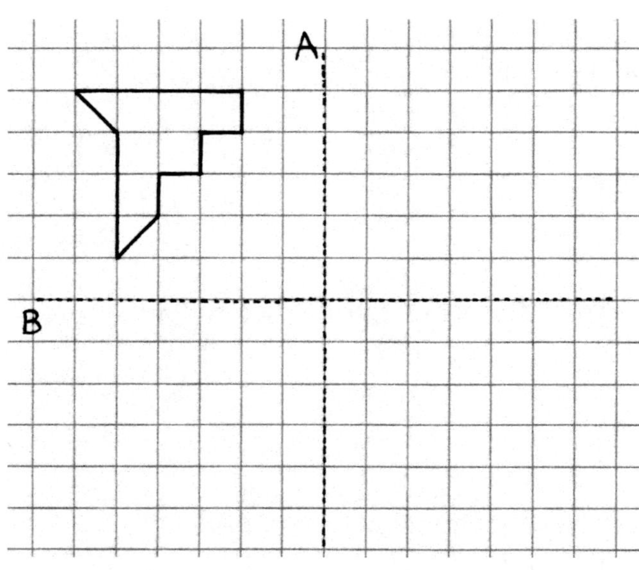

Draw the reflection of the shape in mirror line A.

Draw the reflection of the shape in mirror line B.

19. A, B, C, D, E and F represent digits between 0 and 9 inclusive. A, B and C are different digits, and A is the biggest, e.g. 631 or 927.

By choosing digits for A, B and C, find the answer to

$$
\begin{array}{r}
A\ B\ C \\
-\ C\ B\ A \\
\hline
D\ E\ F \\
+\ F\ E\ D \\
\hline
\end{array}
$$

____

20.

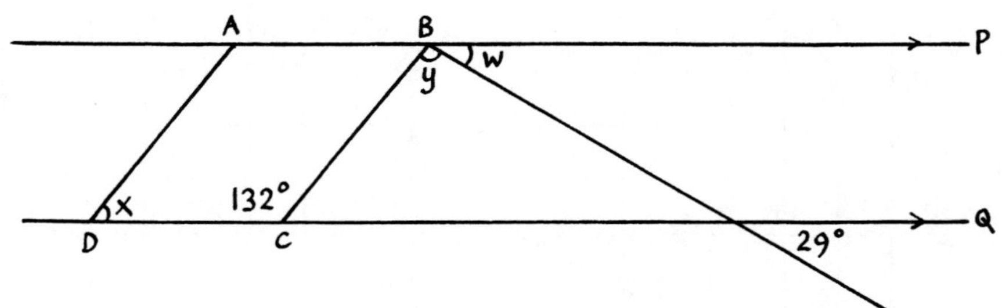

Lines P and Q are parallel. ABCD is a parallelogram (*not drawn accurately*).

Calculate the sizes of angles w, x and y.

w _____________   x _____________   y _____________

21. I am exactly half way through my working day which started at 8.40 a.m. and will finish
at 5.30 p.m. What time is it now?

____

22. What is

(a) the square of the cube of 2 ?

____

(b) the square of $\frac{3}{4}$?

____

(c) the cube of the square of -1 ?

____

23. A map is drawn with a scale of 1:5 000.

(a) The length of a garden on the map is 35 mm. How long, in metres, is the real garden?

____

(b) A footpath is 260 m long. What is its length, in millimetres, on the map?

____

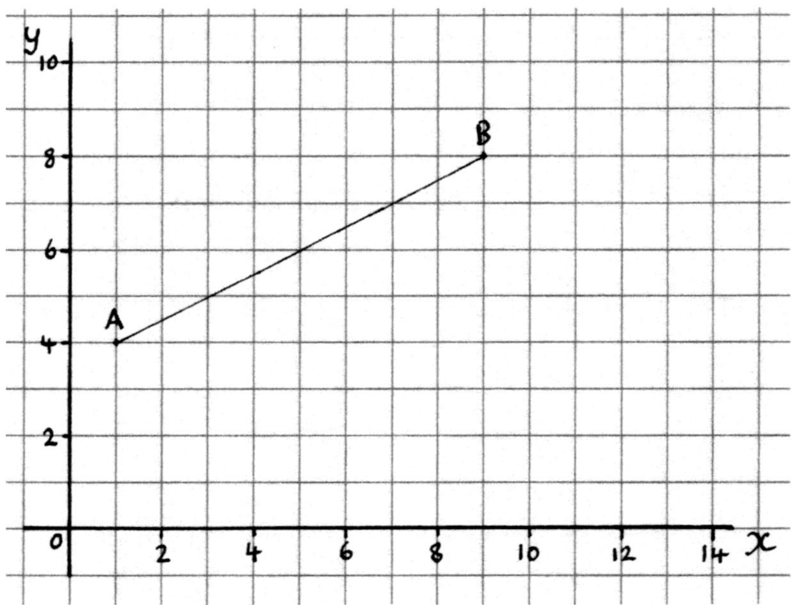

Gradient $= \dfrac{\text{how far up}}{\text{how far along}} = \dfrac{y}{x}$

Gradient of AB is $\dfrac{4}{8} = \dfrac{1}{2} = 50\%$

Plot points C (9 , 6) , D (4 , 3) and E (13 , 6).

Express the gradient of each of these as a percentage to the nearest whole number.

AC

Gradient of AC is

____

DE

Gradient of DE is

____

AE

Gradient of AE is

____

25. John visits his Aunt Willow every 4 days, Mandy visits her every 6 days and Sue visits her every 9 days. They all visit her today. How long will it be before they all visit her on the same day again?

____

26. Kieran is three years older than Myles and five years younger than Ronan. The sum of their ages is 53.

How old is Kieran?

____

27.

degrees	45°W	30°W	15°W	0°	15°E	30°E	45°E	degrees
hours	−3	−2	−1	0	+1	+2	+3	hours

0
LONDON

For every 15° east or west of London, the time changes by 1 hour. East of London the time is later; west of London the time is earlier.

Example: Catania (Sicily) is 15° E of London. If the time in London is 10:00, the time in Catania is   10:00 + 1 hour = 11:00.

When the time in London is 14:00, what time is it in these places?

(a) Alexandria (Egypt)   30° E

____

(b) Denver (U.S.A.)   105° W

____

(c) Muéo (New Caledonia)   165° E

____

(d) When the time is 05:30 in Memphis (U.S.A.), it is 11:30 in London. How many degrees west of London is Memphis?

____

28. Krishna bats in seven cricket matches. His scores (numbers of runs) in the first six matches are
$$12 \ , \ 0 \ , \ 14 \ , \ 3 \ , \ 17 \ , \ 8$$

(a) What is his average (mean) score for the first six matches?

____

(b) How many runs does he have to score in the seventh match to increase his average score by 1 ?

____

29.

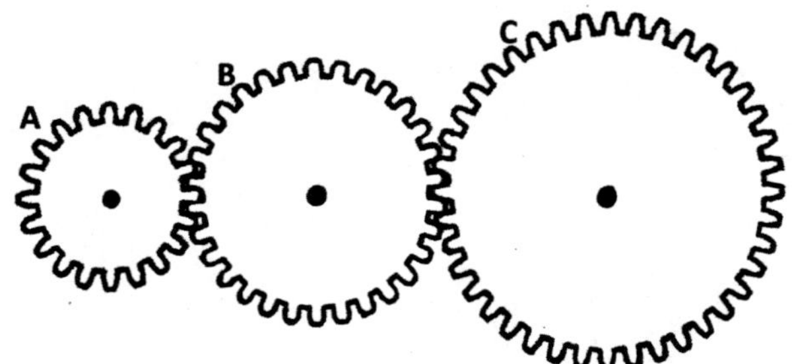

Three gear wheels **A**, **B** and **C** have 20, 30 and 40 teeth respectively. Wheel **A** drives wheel **B** which drives wheel **C**.

When **A** rotates 12 times (makes 12 complete revolutions) clockwise

(a) how many revolutions does **B** make, and in which direction (clockwise or anticlockwise)?

Number of revolutions ________   Direction ____________________________

(b) how many revolutions does **C** make, and in which direction?

Number of revolutions ________   Direction ____________________________

30. Gregg and Nev plan to drive their cars on a journey of 2 520 miles.

Gregg's car goes 63 miles for every gallon of petrol.
Nev's car goes 45 miles for every gallon of petrol.

Nev's car will need more petrol than Gregg's to complete the journey. How many gallons more?

____

END OF PAPER G

1. To what number does the arrow point in each of these?

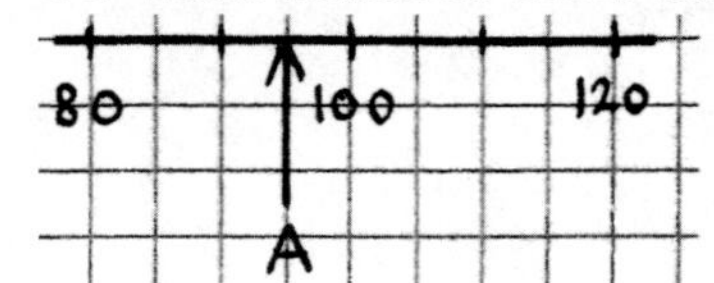 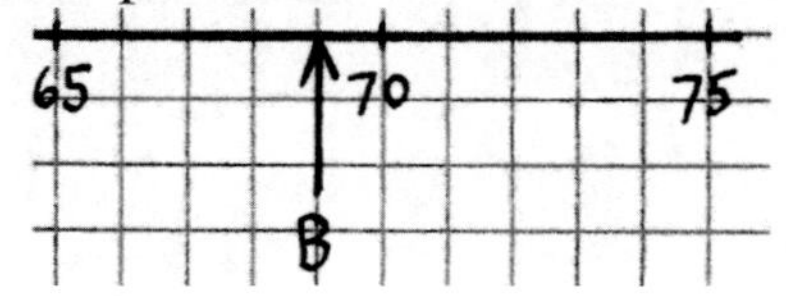 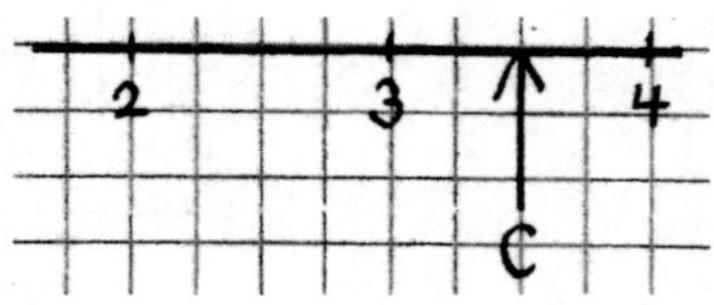

A = _______________   B = _______________   C = _______________

2.
```
      7 1
    1 8 5
  +   6 2
  _______
```

____

3. Write the correct number in each empty square.

(a) 90 ÷ ☐ = 5   (b) ☐ − 12 = −3   (c) 4 × ☐ = 92

4. Multiply 143 by 54.

____

5. Share £1032 equally between 16 people.

____

6. Write the next two numbers in each of these sequences.

(a) 999 , 966 , 933 , _______ , _______

(b) 7 , 10 , 9 , 12 , 11 , 14 , _______ , _______

7. How many seconds are there between 9.00 a.m. and 10.15 a.m.?

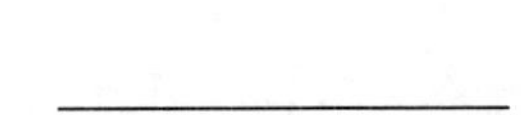

____

8.

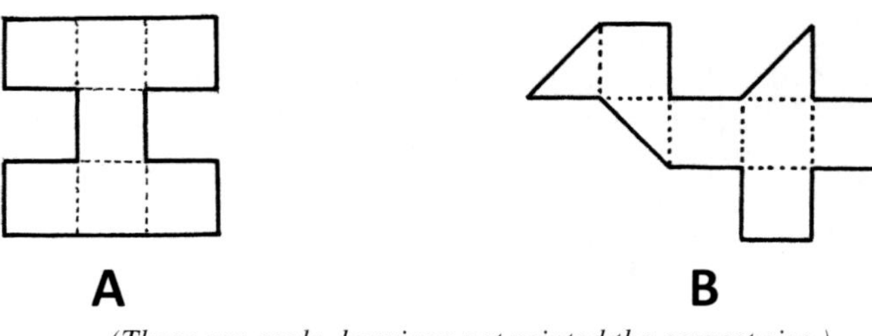

A   **B**

(These are scale drawings not printed the correct size.)

Each of the squares in figure A has an area of 9cm².
Calculate the perimeter of the figure.

____

Figure B is made up of squares and half squares. Each square is 4cm long.
Calculate the area of the figure.

____

9. Simplify

(a) $6 \div \dfrac{3}{4}$ (b) $\dfrac{1}{2} \times \dfrac{5}{6} \times 9$ (c) $\dfrac{5}{6} + \dfrac{1}{2} - \dfrac{1}{3}$

__________   __________   __________

10. Ryan has 87 pence.

(a) What is the highest numbers of coins he could have?

____

(b) What is the lowest number of coins he could have?

____

11. If $d = 4$, $e = 9$, find the values of

(i) $3d + 2e$ (ii) $d - e$ (iii) $\dfrac{e}{6d}$ (iv) $\sqrt{d + e + de}$

________   ________   ________   ________

12.

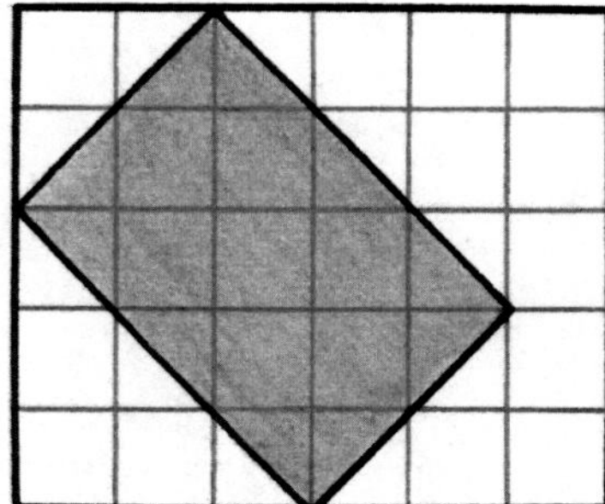

(a) What fraction of the large rectangle is the coloured rectangle?

____

(b) How many more squares should be coloured so that one third of the large rectangle remains white?

____

13. Tammy has 73p , Ruth has 18p and Nancy has 23p.

(a) How much would Tammy have to give to the others so that they all had the same amount?

____

(b) By how much would Ruth's amount have increased?

____

14.

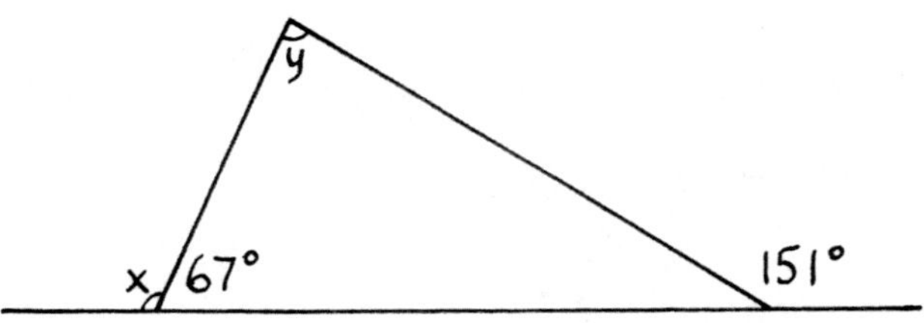

(a) Find the size of angle x.

(b) Find the size of angle y.

_____________   _____________

15. There are three classes of ticket on a certain airline from London to Moscow. Prices of First Class, Business Class and Economy Class are in the ratio 3 : 2 : 1.
The cost of 8 Economy tickets is £6 800.

Five friends travel from London to Moscow. Three travel First Class; the other two travel Business Class. What is the total cost of their tickets?

____

16. (a) Add together   2·7
half of 2·7
a third of 2·7
a tenth of 2·7
a hundredth of 2·7

____

(b) Multiply your answer to (a) by 1000.

____

17.

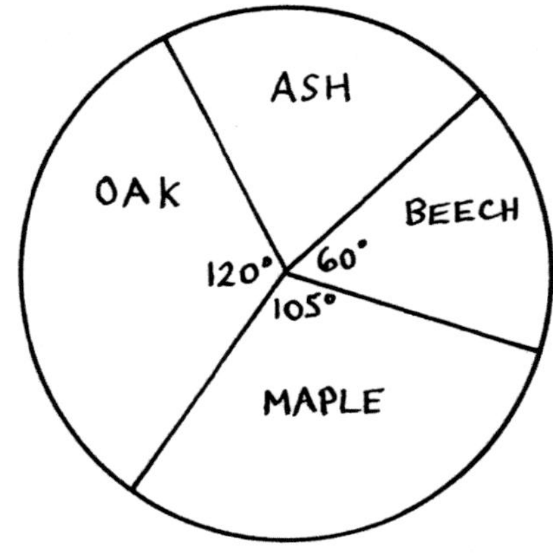

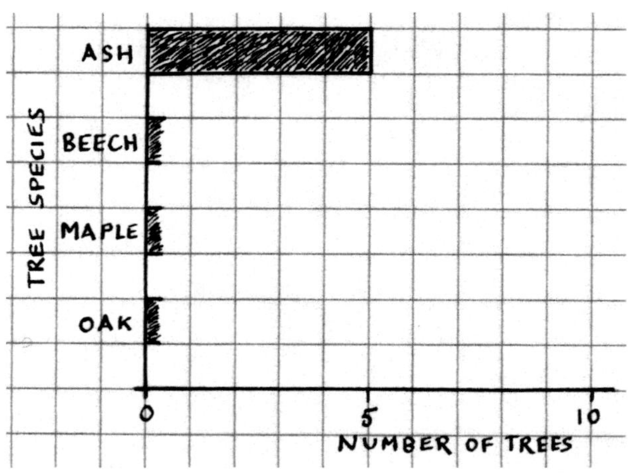

The pie chart shows the different kinds of tree growing in a small wood of 24 trees.

(a) What angle should be written in the ASH sector?

____

(b) Complete the bar chart to show the same information.

18. During a sale, a clothes shop sells all its goods at 70% of the original price.

(a) A sweater originally cost £22.00. How much does it cost in the sale?

____

(b) In the sale, a pair of trainers costs £21.00. What was the original price?

____

19.

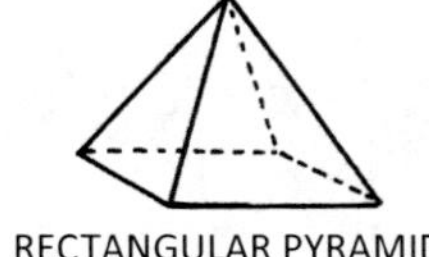

RECTANGULAR PYRAMID

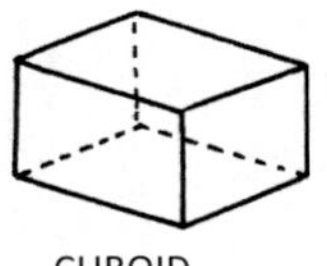

CUBOID

(i) A pyramid with a rectangular base has 5 faces.

How many vertices (corners) does it have?   How many edges does it have?

_______   _______

(ii) A cuboid has 8 vertices.

How many faces does it have?   How many edges does it have?

_______   _______

(iii) These two solids follow Euler's formula: faces + vertices = edges + 2.

A convex icosahedron also follows this formula. It has 20 faces and 12 vertices. How many edges does it have?

____

20. The difference between the squares of two single-digit numbers is 39. What is the sum of the numbers?

____

21. The area of the base of a cylindrical bucket is 450 cm². The height of the bucket is 24 cm. How many litres will it hold?

____

22. Given that ❖ + 1 = ☐, write out this subtraction again, replacing the signs with the correct digits.

```
    ☐ ❖ 2 7            2 7
  - 1 5 ★ ❖          - 1 5
  _________          _______
    2 7 ★ ☐            2 7
```

23.

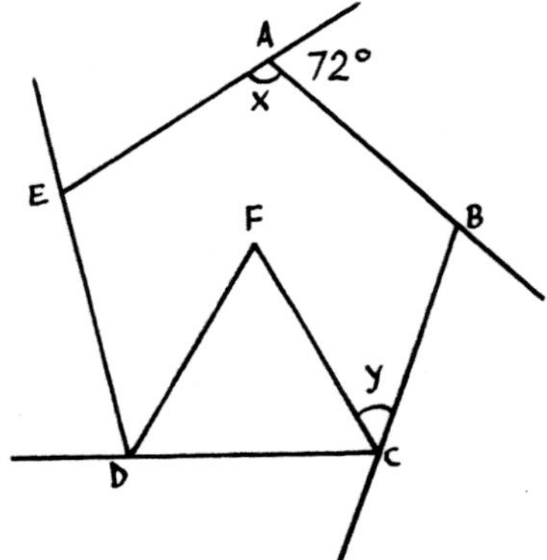

ABCDE is a regular pentagon. CDF is an
equilateral triangle.

(i) What size is angle x ?

____

(ii) What size is angle y ?

____

24. A temperature of 0° Celsius (0°C) is equivalent to 273° Kelvin (273°K).
1 degree Kelvin = 1 degree Celsius.

(a) Water boils at 100°C. What temperature is this in °K ?

____

(b) Average human body temperature is 37°C. How much is this in °K ?

____

(c) The lowest recorded outside temperature in the U.K. (up to the year 2015) is 246°K.
Convert this temperature to °C.

____

25. I always buy my cereal, squash and bread on the same day. A packet of cereal lasts me
8 days, a bottle of squash lasts me 12 days, and a bread loaf lasts me 6 days.

How many bread loaves do I have to buy to last me until I shop for these items again?

____

26. Each of 141, 108, 81, 144, 78 and 114, when multiplied by the same single-digit
number, gives a three-digit answer containing identical digits but in different orders. The
sum of the answers is 3996.

What is the number?

____

27.

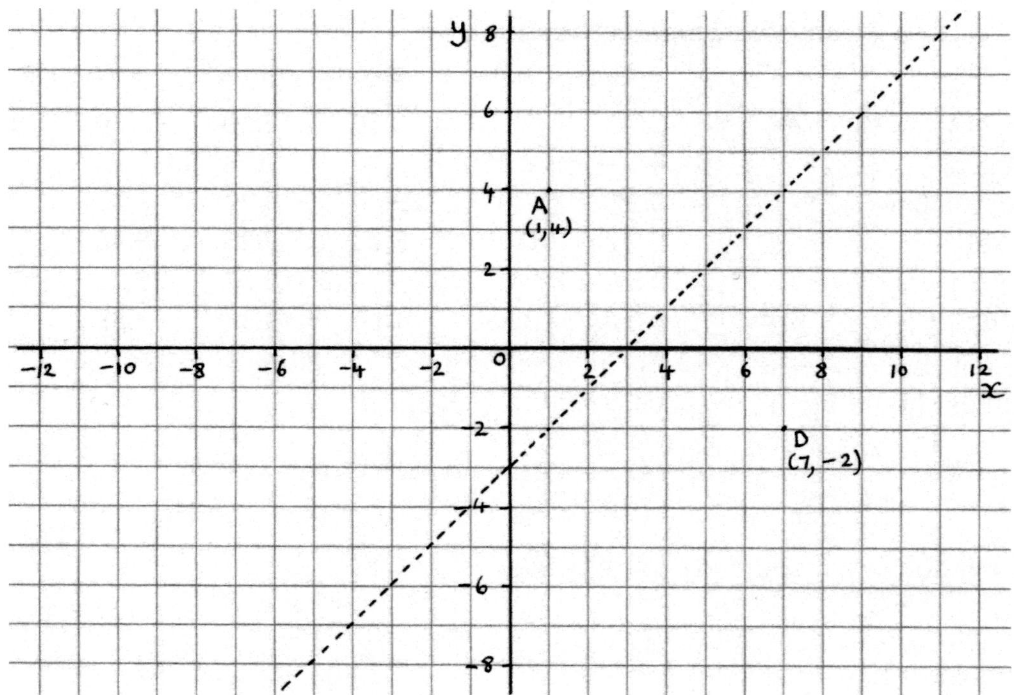

The grid shows the points A (1 , 4) and D (7 , –2).

Plot points B (4 , 6) and C (4 , 1). Join ABC to make a triangle. Write letter T inside the triangle.

Reflect triangle T in the y axis. Write letter V in the new triangle.

Reflect triangle T in the dotted line. Write W in the new triangle.

Point E lies on the dotted line. CE is the same length as AD. What could be the coordinates of E ? Give the two possible answers.

Coordinates of E are either ______________ or ______________

28. Jonty has a sack containing green apples and red apples. There are 36 apples altogether, of which 20 are green.

(a) Without looking in the sack, he takes out an apple. What is the probability that it will be red?

____

(b) The apple is red. Jonty keeps it and, without looking, he takes another apple from the sack. What is the probability that it will be red ?

____

29. The timetable shows five journeys of a bus service from Market Westwick to Thornburn, calling at four villages in between.

		a.m.	a.m.	a.m.	a.m.	a.m.
Market Westwick	*depart*	8.10	8.30	8.50	9.10	9.30
Folkfield		8.16	8.36	8.56	**C**	9.36
Hampton Bay		8.22	**A**	9.02	9.22	9.42
Blacketby		8.25	8.45	9.05	9.25	9.45
Albertgates		8.31	8.51	**B**	9.31	9.51
Thornburn	*arrive*	8.38	8.58	9.18	9.38	9.58

(i) What times should be in the spaces marked **A**, **B** and **C** ?

> **A** __________   **B** __________   **C** __________

(ii) How long does each complete journey take?

> __________

(iii) Bus times are similar all through the day. A bus arrives at Thornburn at 12.18 p.m. At what time did it depart from Market Westwick?

> __________

(iv) Folkfield is $4\frac{1}{4}$ miles from Albertgates. What is the speed of the bus between these two villages in miles/hour (m.p.h.) ?

> __________

30.

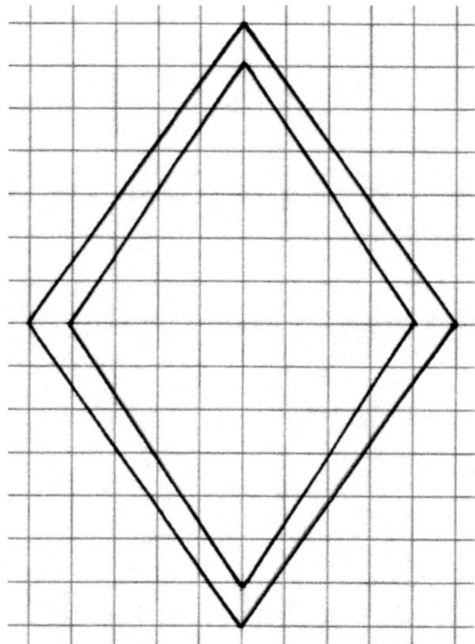

The diagram shows a rhombus within another rhombus. What is the area, in square units, of the space between the two rhombuses? (Each red square has a length of 1 unit.)

> __________

END OF PAPER H

1.
```
      5 5 1
    2 5 6 3
  +   3 2 0
  ─────────
```

2.
```
    8 3 0 7
  − 3 9 6 4
  ─────────
```

3. 418 × 8

4. 3906 ÷ 9

5. Write numbers in the squares to make the sequences correct.

4   6   9   ☐   18   24   ☐

13   9   5   ☐   −3   ☐

6. A film lasted 1 hour 38 minutes. It ended at 9.11 p.m.

(a) At what time did it start?

(b) At what time, in 24-hour clock, did it end?

7. Write these fractions in order of size, starting with the smallest.

$$\frac{4}{9} \, , \quad \frac{2}{5} \, , \quad \frac{9}{20} \, , \quad \frac{3}{7}$$

8.

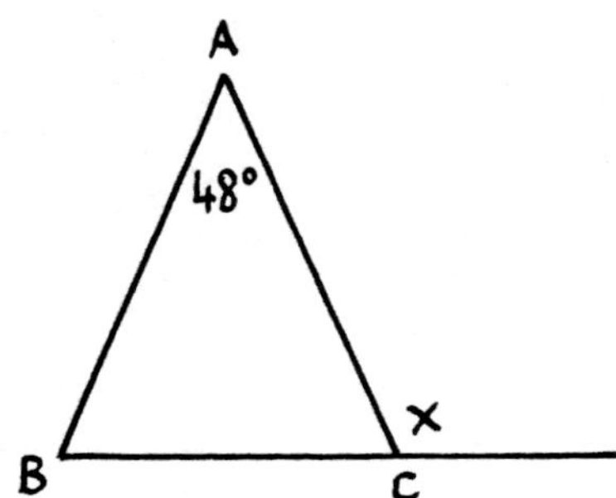

AB and AC are equal in length.

Find the size of angle x.

____

9. Sophie has 40 toffees. She gives $\frac{1}{5}$ of them to Eva, $\frac{1}{4}$ of them to Mia and $\frac{3}{8}$ of them to Annabel. How many toffees does she keep for herself?

____

10. Find the sum of   9·005 , 11·32 , 3 and 0·54

____

11. Mr Goodbody's oil tank holds 1100 litres of oil. It is three quarters full.

If he uses 5 litres of oil each day, how many days will it be before the tank is empty?

____

12.

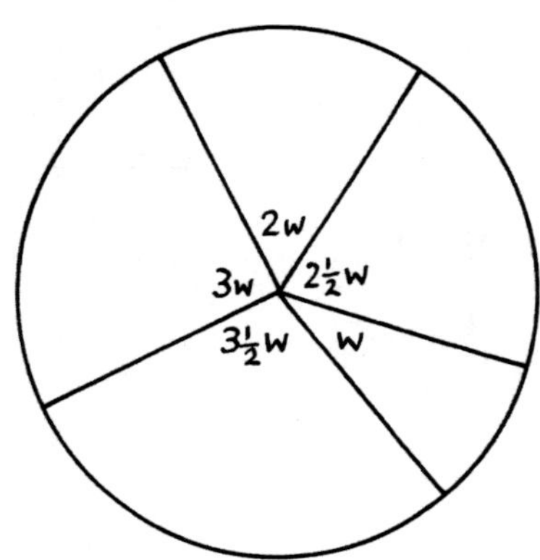

The diagram shows angle sizes in a pie chart (not drawn accurately).

Find the value of w (in degrees).

____

13. (a) Multiply 86 by 34.

From your answer (or otherwise), find

(b) 8600 × 340

(c) 0·86 × 3·4

14.

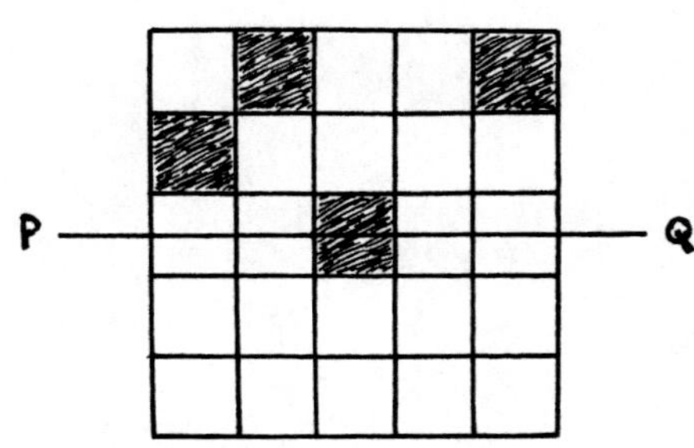

(a) What percentage of the large square is shaded?

(b) Shade three more small squares so that the large square is symmetrical about the line PQ.

(c) What percentage of the large square is now shaded?

15. Find the value of m in each of these equations.

(i) $7m + 5m - m = 22$

(ii) $6m = 4m + 18$

(iii) $\dfrac{m}{3} + \dfrac{m}{4} + \dfrac{m}{6} = 48$

16.

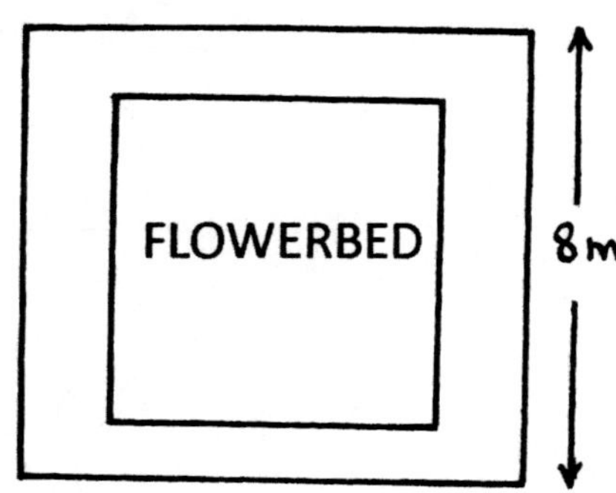

A square flowerbed 6 metres long is dug out of a lawn 8 metres wide.

The area of the flowerbed is now the same as the remaining lawn.

How long is the lawn?

____

17.   (a) $4 - 3\frac{5}{8}$

(b) $\frac{5}{6} + \frac{1}{15} - \frac{7}{10}$

_______________   _______________

18. The currency of the imaginary country of Kavyova is the Kavyovan dollar (KA$).

Today, £1.00 equals KA$1.40 (1 pound equals 1·4 Kavyovan dollars).

(a) Find the value of £19.00 in Kavyovan dollars.

____

(b) Find the value of KA$420 in pounds.

____

19.

Each line, each column and each diagonal adds up to 6w . What number should be in the square with the question mark?

	?	
		2w
	4w	w

____

20. During the afternoon the outside temperature was 5·3° C. By midnight it had fallen by 8·5° C. What was the midnight temperature?

____

21.

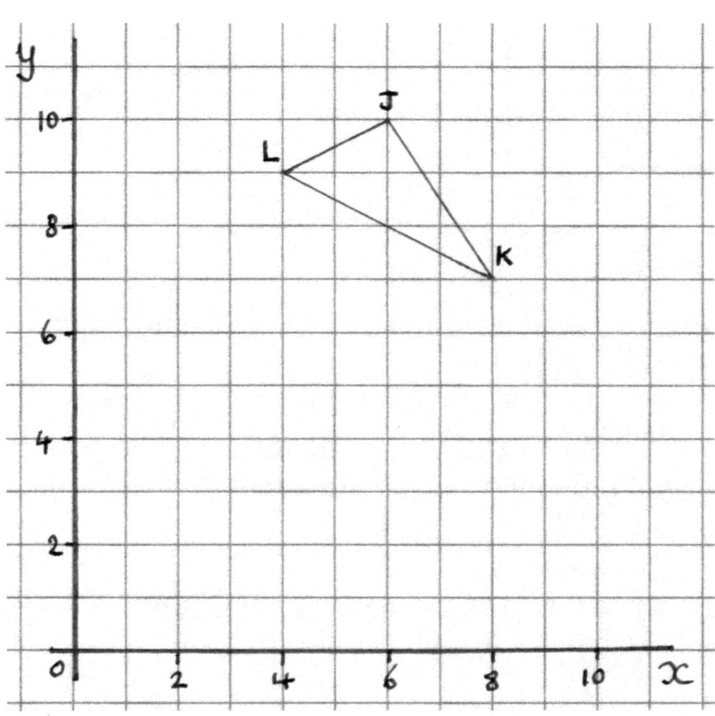

(i) Write down the coordinates of point K.

____

(ii) Produce (extend) JK to M so that KM is the same length as JK.

(iii) Produce JL to N so that LN is the same length as JL.

(iv) Write down the coordinates of the mid-point of MN.

____

(v) What is the ratio of the area of the triangle JKL to the area of the trapezium LKMN ?

____

22. There were 96 crows, 78 gulls and 116 pigeons in a field. Half of the pigeons and a third of the crows flew away. What percentage of the remaining birds were pigeons?

____

23.

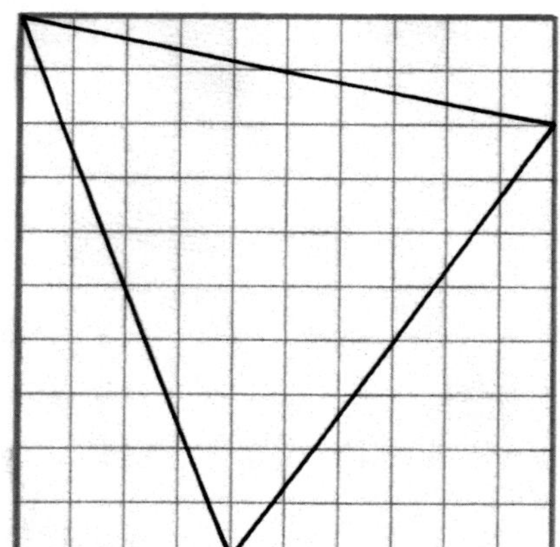

What is the area, in square units, of the black triangle? (Each red square has a length of 1 unit.)

____

24. Dave recorded the air pressure, in millibars, each day of a certain week:-

Monday	995 mb	Friday	1006 mb
Tuesday	996 mb	Saturday	?
Wednesday	1004 mb	Sunday	1015 mb
Thursday	1008 mb		

The average (mean) daily pressure for the week was 1005 mb. What pressure did he record on Saturday?

____

25. (a) Copy this sum, replacing ★ and ☐ with the correct digits (★ and ☐ are two different digits).

```
    5  ★  ★  ☐
 +  2  ★  ☐  ☐           +
   ___________          ________
    ☐  ★  ☐  6
```

(b) A three-digit number with digits H H H is multiplied by a two-digit number H H . The result is 59 829. Which digit does H stand for?

____

26. In a farmyard there are dogs and hens. Altogether there are 16 heads and 38 legs.

(a) How many dogs are there?

____

(b) How many hens are there?

____

27. Layla and Victoria go on an 11 mile charity walk.

Layla sets off from school at 2.00 p.m. and walks at 3 miles an hour (m.p.h.).
Victoria sets off from school at 2.45 p.m. and walks at 4 miles an hour.

(a) At what time does Victoria catch up with Layla?

____

(b) How far are they from school?

____

(c) They continue the walk together, going at Layla's speed. At what time do they finish the walk?

____

28.

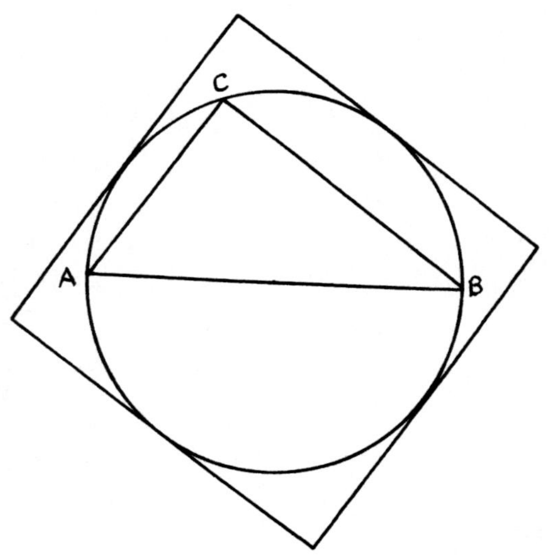

Points A, B and C lie on the circumference of the circle.

AB is a diameter of the circle whose radius is 5 cm.

The circle fits exactly into the square.
AC = 6 cm, BC = 8 cm.

Express the perimeter of triangle ABC as a fraction of the perimeter of the square.

____

29. There are six different arrangements of the digits 1, 6 and 9.

169   196   619   691   916   961

(i) 169 is the square of a number with digits AB. What digits do A and B stand for ?

A   B
_______   _______

(ii) One of the six arrangements is the square of the number with digits BA. Which of the arrangements is it ?

____

(iii) Which **two** of the arrangements are prime numbers ?

and
______________   ______________

(iv) Apart from the squares in (i) and (ii), another of the arrangements is a square. Which arrangement is it, and what number is it the square of ?

is the square of
______________   ________

30. There were 122 passengers on an airliner. All were either British or French.

80 were married; 73 were French; 51 of the French passengers were married.

How many unmarried British passengers were on the airliner?

____

END OF PAPER J

1. Find the missing numbers in these sequences.

(a)   4 ,   10 ,   _______ ,   22 ,   _______ ,   34

(b)   40 ,   20 ,   _______ ,   5 ,   _______ ,   _______

2.

```
    1  2  3  5
 -     5  8  1
   ___________
```

____

3. Copy this sum, replacing * and Δ with the correct numbers.

```
    1  *  Δ  9              1        9
 +  5  6  *  Δ           +  5  6
   __________               __________
    *  Δ  2  3                    2  3
```

4. Multiply 1646 by 6.

____

5. The square of 8 is 64. By dividing by 8 and then by 8 again (or by any other method), work out 269632 ÷ 64.

____

6. Write in figures: two million fifty six thousand and nine

____

7. $\frac{5}{8}$ of a number equals 20. What is the number?

____

8. These fractions all have an equal value. Complete the empty squares with the correct numbers.

$$\frac{\square}{9} = \frac{8}{12} = \frac{\square}{30} = \frac{12}{\square}$$

9.

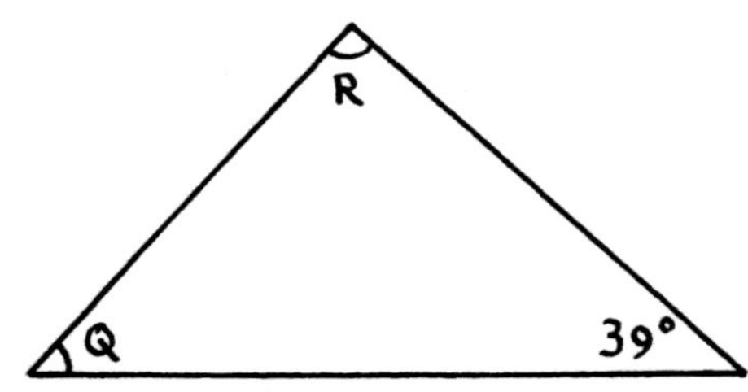

In this triangle (*not drawn to scale*), angle R is twice the size of angle Q. Calculate the sizes of angles Q and R.

Angle Q =

____

Angle R =

____

10. $1{\cdot}627 - 0{\cdot}34 + 1{\cdot}066$

____

11. Write

(a) $\frac{3}{4}$ as a decimal.

____

(b) $0{\cdot}61$ as a percentage.

____

(c) 35% as a fraction in its lowest terms.

____

12. Maxim lives in Oak Road which has 32 houses numbered 1 to 32.

The number of Maxim's house is 1 less than a multiple of 5. It divides by 3 and is 1 more than a prime number.

Which number is Maxim's house?

____

13.   **6 2 4 · 7 3**

In this number what is the value of

(a) 2   (b*) 3   (c) 6   (d*) 7

________   ________   ________   ________

* Give answers to (b) and (d) as fractions.

14. To balance a beam, the mass times the distance (M x D) on one side of the fulcrum (balancing point) equals the mass times the distance on the other side.

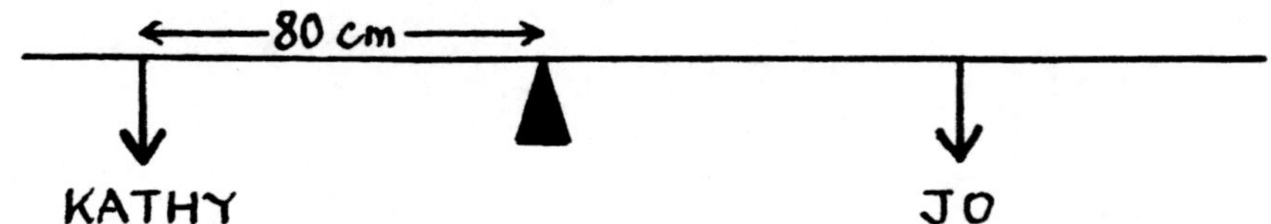

Kathy weighs 35 kg. She sits on the left side of the beam 80 cm from the balancing point.

Her sister Jo weighs 25 kg. How far to the right of the balancing point must she sit to balance the beam?   (Do not bother about how much the beam weighs.)

____

15.   (a) $\dfrac{3}{4}$ + $\dfrac{7}{20}$ − $\dfrac{1}{5}$ =

______

(b) $1\dfrac{4}{11}$ × $\dfrac{2}{3}$ × $4\dfrac{1}{8}$ =

______

16. A group of 11 people went on holiday together. Their ages were

14   11   19   13   11   9   14   10   11   19   12

Find which age was (a) the mode.

______

(b) the median.

______

(c) the mean (average).

______

17.

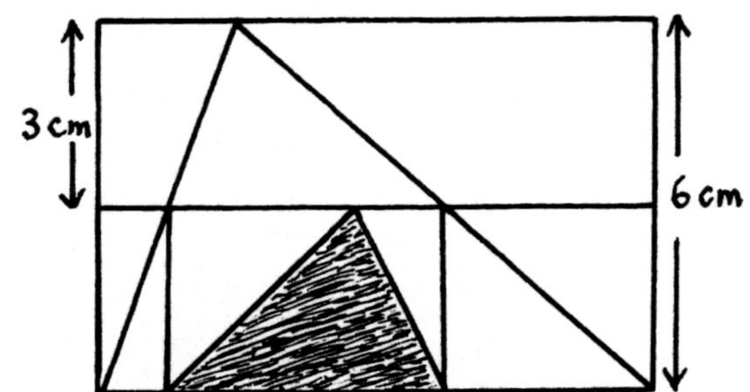

The perimeter of the large rectangle is 44 cm.

What is the area of the shaded triangle?

____

18.   Find the value of

[a] $(8 - 3) \times 4$

____

[b] $2 + 6 \times 5$

____

[c] $4 + 7 \times 3 - 10$

____

[d] $18 \div (11 - 8)$

____

19. Two numbers added together make 61. When the smaller number is subtracted from the larger number, the result is 15.

What are the two numbers?

_______________ and _______________

20. If $n = 2$ and $p = 7$, what are the values of

(i) $5n - 2p$

____

(ii) $3np$

____

(iii) $p^2 + n^2$

____

21.

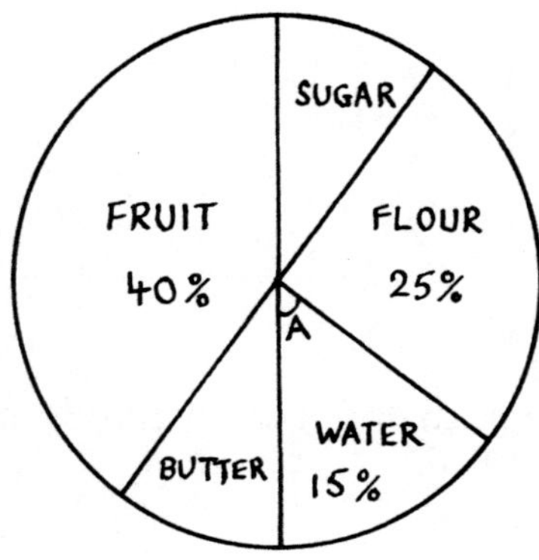

The main ingredients for Aunt Ellen's fruit cake are shown in the pie chart.

There are equal amounts of sugar and butter. The flour weighs (has a mass of) 150 g.

(a) What is the size of angle A?

____

(b) What is the total mass (weight) of the cake?

____

(c) What percentage of the cake is butter?

____

(d) How much does the fruit weigh?

____

22. Tank A is a cuboid with base 24 cm long and 12 cm wide, and a height of y cm.
Tank B is a cuboid with a square base y cm long, and a height of 18 cm.

Both tanks have the same volume. Find the value of y.

____

23.

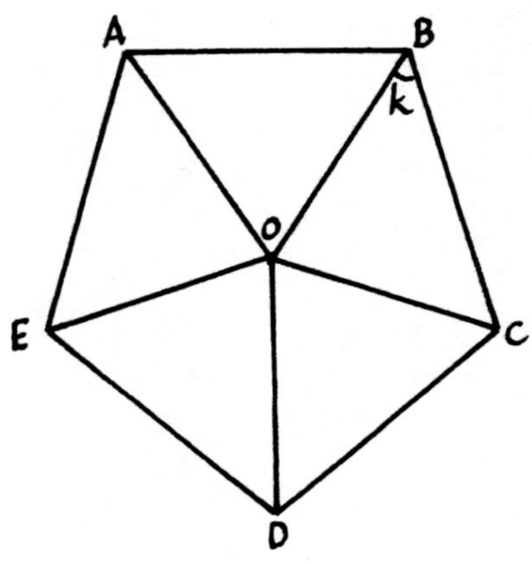

O is the centre of the regular pentagon ABCDE (*not drawn accurately*).

Calculate the size of angle k.

____

24. [100cm = 1m;   1000m = 1km]

(a) How many centimetres (cm) are there in 1 kilometre (km) ?

____

A map is drawn to a scale of 1 : 20 000.

(b) Two villages are 11 cm apart on the map. What is the real distance between them in km ?

____

(c) My friend Tyler's house is 3 km away from mine. What would the distance be, in cm, between our houses on the map?

____

25. A is 80% of B.

Express B as a percentage of A.

____

26.

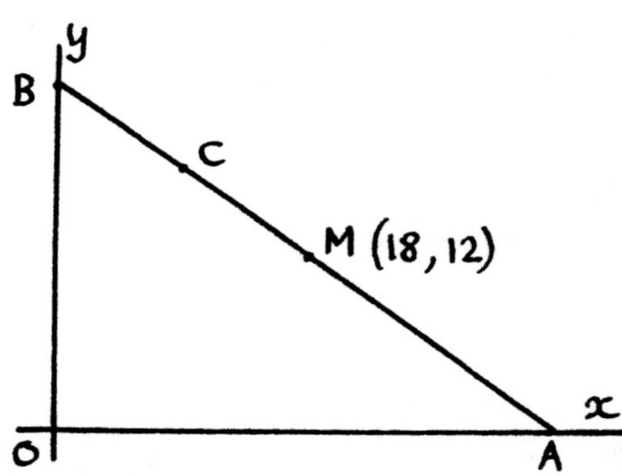

M is the mid-point of the line AB. What are the coordinates of A?

(_____ , _____)

C is the mid-point of MB. What are the coordinates of C?

(_____ , _____)

27. A bus company has double-deck buses for hire. Each bus holds 77 people.

(a) A group of 295 people want to hire buses to take them on a day trip.
How many buses will they need?

____

The bus company also has minibuses for hire. Each minibus holds 16 people.

(b) If the group decide to hire a mixture of double-deckers and minibuses, how many of
each will they need to hire so that there are no spare places in any of the buses?

_________ double-deckers and _________ minibuses

28. The digits 2, 5 and 9 can be arranged to make six different numbers

259   295   529   592   925   952

(a) Which two of the numbers, when added together, make 1481 ?

_________ and _________

(b) The difference between two of the numbers is 630. What are the two numbers?

_________ and _________

(c) 259, 592 and 925 are all multiples of the same number (apart from 1). What is the
number?

____

(d) Which of the numbers is a square?

____

29.

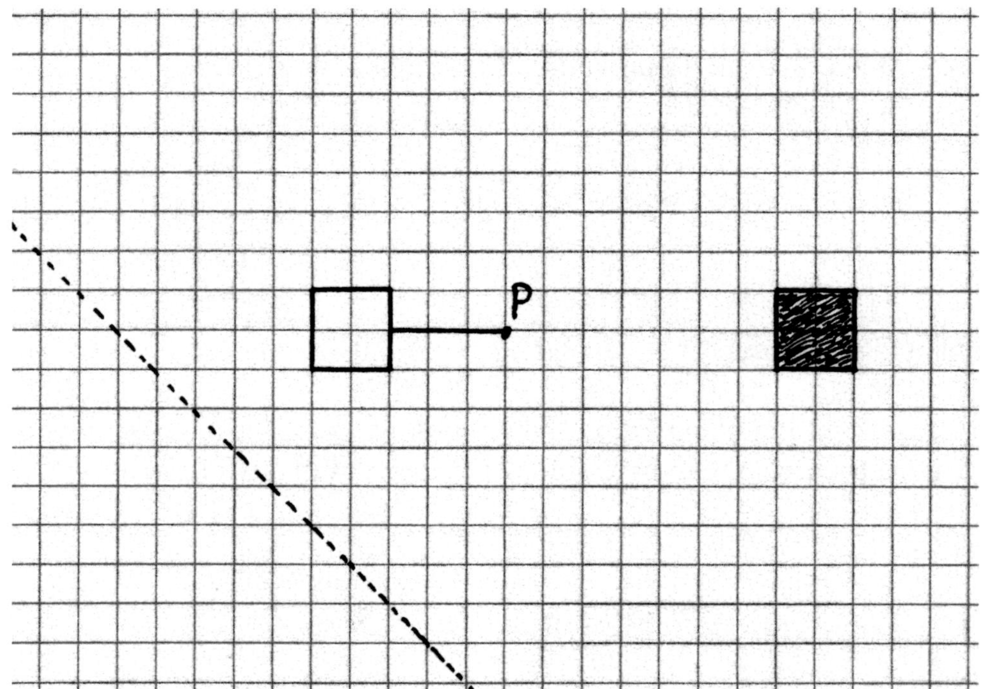

Draw the mirror line (line of symmetry) which makes the shaded box a reflection of the white box.

Rotate the white box 90° clockwise about point P. Write the letter A in the new box.

Reflect the white box in the dotted line. Write the letter B in the new box.

When box A is rotated 180° about point K, it maps on to the shaded box. Mark point K in the correct position.

30. Cragstone Castle charges £12 admission for each adult and £7 for each child.

On a certain day, 230 people visited the castle and the total amount paid by all the visitors was £2 460.

How many children visited the castle?

END OF PAPER K